Suddenly the Shadow

Leslie Meisels

WITH A SHORT MEMOIR BY HIS WIFE, EVA MEISELS,
AND AN INTRODUCTION BY ANNA PORTER

THE AZRIELI FOUNDATION
www.azrielifoundation.org

Cover and book design by Mark Goldstein
Endpaper maps by Martin Gilbert
Map on page xxvii by François Blanc

LIBRARY AND ARCHIVES CANADA CATALOGUING IN PUBLICATION

Meisels, Leslie, 1927–, author
    Suddenly the shadow fell/ Leslie Meisels.

(The Azrieli series of Holocaust survivor memoirs; Series VI)
Includes bibliographical references and index.
ISBN 978-1-897470-42-8 (pbk.)

1. Meisels, Leslie, 1927–. 2. Meisels, Leslie, 1927–, Family. 3. Holocaust, Jewish (1939–1945) – Hungary – Personal narratives. 4. Jewish ghettos – Hungary – Na´dudvar – History – 20th century. 5. World War, 1939–1945 – Conscript labor – Austria. 6. Bergen-Belsen (Concentration camp). 7. Holocaust survivors – Canada – Biography. I. Azrieli Foundation, issuing body II. Title. III. Series: Azrieli series of Holocaust survivor memoirs. Series; VI

DS135.H93M45 2014   940.53'18092   C2014-900932-1

PRINTED IN CANADA

The Azrieli Series of Holocaust Survivor Memoirs

Contents

Series Preface:
In their own words...

In telling these stories, the writers have liberated themselves. For so many years we did not speak about it, even when we became free people living in a free society. Now, when at last we are writing about what happened to us in this dark period of history, knowing that our stories will be read and live on, it is possible for us to feel truly free. These unique historical documents put a face on what was lost, and allow readers to grasp the enormity of what happened to six million Jews – one story at a time.

David J. Azrieli, C.M., C.Q., M.Arch
Holocaust survivor and founder, The Azrieli Foundation

Since the end of World War II, over 30,000 Jewish Holocaust survivors have immigrated to Canada. Who they are, where they came from, what they experienced and how they built new lives for themselves and their families are important parts of our Canadian heritage. The Azrieli Foundation's Holocaust Survivor Memoirs Program was established to preserve and share the memoirs written by those who survived the twentieth-century Nazi genocide of the Jews of Europe and later made their way to Canada. The program is guided by the conviction that each survivor of the Holocaust has a remarkable story to tell, and that such stories play an important role in education about tolerance and diversity.

Millions of individual stories are lost to us forever. By preserving the stories written by survivors and making them widely available to a broad audience, the Azrieli Foundation's Holocaust Survivor Memoirs Program seeks to sustain the memory of all those who perished at the hands of hatred, abetted by indifference and apathy. The personal accounts of those who survived against all odds are as different as the people who wrote them, but all demonstrate the courage, strength, wit and luck that it took to prevail and survive in such terrible adversity. The memoirs are also moving tributes to people – strangers and friends – who risked their lives to help others, and who, through acts of kindness and decency in the darkest of moments, frequently helped the persecuted maintain faith in humanity and courage to endure. These accounts offer inspiration to all, as does the survivors' desire to share their experiences so that new generations can learn from them.

The Holocaust Survivor Memoirs Program collects, archives and publishes these distinctive records and the print editions are available free of charge to libraries, educational institutions and Holocaust-education programs across Canada. They are also available for sale to the general public at bookstores.

The Azrieli Foundation would like to express appreciation to the following people for their invaluable efforts in producing this book: Sherry Dodson (Maracle Press), Sir Martin Gilbert, Andrea Knight, and Margie Wolfe and Emma Rodgers of Second Story Press.

About the Glossary

The following memoir contains a number of terms, concepts and historical references that may be unfamiliar to the reader. For information on major organizations; significant historical events and people; geographical locations; religious and cultural terms; and foreign-language words and expressions that will help give context and background to the events described in the text, please see the glossary beginning on page 95.

Introduction

The catastrophe of Hungarian Jewry during World War II came late. Its speed and ferocity were unrivalled, as was the unwillingness of those caught up in its maw to foresee its inevitability.

The First Anti-Jewish Law in twentieth-century Europe was introduced in Hungary as early as 1923 but, given that Jews had been relatively well integrated into Hungarian society since the latter half of the nineteenth century, most Hungarian Jews did not consider this to be a serious threat. It limited the number of Jews admitted to universities to 6 per cent, the percentage of Jews in the general population, but it was allowed to lapse eight years later. Nevertheless, it did end up being a harbinger of worse to come.

In the aftermath of World War I, conditions in Hungary changed dramatically. At Trianon, a sideshow to the main treaty negotiations at Versailles that ended the war, Hungary lost two-thirds of its territory and three-fifths of its people. By a stroke of a pen, Transylvania became part of Romania, the Upper Province part of Czechoslovakia and the Bácska area part of Yugoslavia.[1] There is little doubt that Hungary suffered the harshest terms dealt out by the victorious Allies.

---

[1] For more on the treaty, look at Margaret MacMillan, *Paris 1919* (Random House, 2003).

The diminution of the country has haunted Hungarians for the rest of the twentieth century and even the beginning of the twenty-first.

Throughout the 1930s, Hungary developed closer ties to Germany, which shared Hungary's outrage and bitterness over the treaty conditions imposed on both countries. In January 1933, Adolf Hitler, head of the National Socialist Party – the Nazis – became chancellor of Germany. The Nazis established the Geheime Staatspolizei, or Gestapo, with powers to arrest, interrogate and imprison without due process, and violent attacks on Jews in Germany became the norm, not the exception. As antisemitism rose in Germany, the contagion began to spread to other European countries and Jews began to look for safe havens.

Refugees flooded into Hungary. In 1938–1939, following the annexation of Austria and the occupation of Czechoslovakia, between 15,000 and 35,000 of those refugees were Jews from Austria, Germany, Poland and Slovakia. Hungarian Jews, however, still felt that the turmoil would pass them by, that they would be protected by the laws and by their fellow citizens in the place that had been their homeland for a thousand years. Not only were there Jewish politicians, academics, journalists, businessmen, land owners, industrialists, poets, writers, doctors, lawyers, famous actors and impresarios – as there were in Poland and Czechoslovakia – but in Hungary Jews had experienced unprecedented tolerance. When Germany occupied and annexed Austria in 1938, in what the Germans termed a friendly gesture, Hungarian Jews still felt secure. They had fought with honour in World War I, thousands were decorated and wore their medals with pride. Most Jews viewed themselves as Hungarians who, incidentally, were of the Jewish faith. Many of them followed no organized religion at all.

When Germany was awarded the Sudetenland at the infamous Munich conference in September of 1938, the Hungarian press was quick to echo Hitler's demand for "lebensraum" – living space – and it was generally assumed that he would be satisfied with the new

Sudeten territory. Admiral Miklós Horthy, Hungary's interwar and wartime leader, was rewarded for his support for Germany's expansion into Czechoslovakia and Austria when Hitler allowed Hungary to annex part of Magyar-speaking Slovakia and Carpathian Ruthenia, lands taken from Hungary in the Treaty of Trianon.

Jews continued to pay little heed when, in May 1939, the Hungarian parliament enacted a stronger version of the lapsed Anti-Jewish Law that restricted the number of Jews in commercial enterprises, the press, in law, and medicine to no more than 20 per cent. This Second Anti-Jewish Law was an imitation of Germany's Nuremberg Laws and, for the first time, defined Jews in Hungary as a race. It provided for the retirement of all Jewish members of the judiciary, cancelled Jews' right to vote in elections, and provided for the formation of a labour service that would eventually force 150,000 Jewish men into military service without guns or rights. Many members of the Hungarian Jewish elite saw this as an effort to appease both the rising right-wing in Hungary and Hitler, whose views on Jews were known from his popular and rabidly antisemitic book, *Mein Kampf.*

World War II began with the invasion of Poland on September 1, 1939; Warsaw fell to German forces on September 28. Throughout 1939, Jews were murdered in their homes, in synagogues, in the streets; they were bayoneted in village squares, shot into open trenches that they themselves had been forced to dig. Refugees flooding into Hungary told horrific stories of atrocities and, as the months went by, of starvation as Poland's Jews were forced into severely overcrowded ghettos.

By 1940, as the Germans moved farther north into Finland, Denmark and Norway, and south into France, Belgium, Luxembourg and the Netherlands, there were hundreds of thousands of refugees in Europe with nowhere to flee. The United States put such barriers before people desperate to escape that most of them were killed before they succeeded in obtaining the right papers. Australia agreed to accept up to 15,000 Jews as, they said "we have no real racial problems and we are not desirous of importing one." Canada only offered entry for "certain classes of agriculturists," a category that could exclude almost everyone.[2] Holland and Denmark had offered limited asylum but they were soon overrun by the Wehrmacht and fell under German occupation.

After Kristallnacht, in November 1938, British immigration policy eased for Jewish child refugees whose parents were in concentration camps. It allowed British Jewish organizations to set up the *Kindertransport* that brought in about 7,500 children from Germany, Austria, Czechoslovakia and Poland. By September 1939, 80,000 Jewish refugees had been admitted, but when the war broke out, all immigration to Britain from countries under Nazi control was banned. In addition, in British-controlled Palestine, they were determined to enforce their quota on Jewish immigrants and began to blockade ships full of desperate European refugees who were trying to reach Palestine.

Hungary officially joined the Axis alliance of Germany, Japan and fascist Italy in November 1940. Europe's Jews were left with no escape routes.

~

Set against this geopolitical backdrop is Leslie Meisels' compelling story of his family's struggle to deal with rapidly changing and deadly circumstances. Just a few months after his bar mitzvah, in the summer of 1940, his father was called up for military service. He took part in the operation to seize Northern Transylvania from Romania, but fortunately, in August, under German-Italian arbitration, the northern half of Transylvania was returned to Hungary and Lajos Meisels

---

2 You may want to read Irving Abella and Harold Troper's *None is Too Many* (University of Toronto Press, 2012) for greater insight into Canada's refusal to take Jewish refugees.

was able to return home. He was, at that point, still able to work for his non-Jewish employer, who protected Lajos from forced labour service. Soon, though, Leslie was denied his dream of attending high school and had to find a place apprenticing with a master cabinet-maker. The restrictions on Jews began to close off all possibilities for employment and education.

The "Jewish problem" or "Jewish question," meanwhile, was regularly debated in parliament where the proportion of radical right-wingers had risen to 20 per cent. Yet most Hungarian Jews appeared to remain unperturbed. They were, after all, patriots. Some business owners found silent gentile partners who would allow them to continue running their enterprises and journalists continued to write under assumed names. They believed this was a phase that would pass and life would return to normal. Many still trusted in Horthy's good will and were sure he had been forced to make a gesture to appease Hitler. The National Bureau of Hungarian Jews was cautioning against public protests. Its president, Samuel Stern, was still a *hofrat*, a court or privy councillor appointed by the Austro-Hungarian Emperor, and a social friend of the regent, Admiral Horthy.

In April 1941, using Hungary as its base of operations, the German army invaded Yugoslavia with the active assistance of the Hungarian army. In July that year, Hermann Göring, president of the Reichstag, issued a directive "for the implementation of the Final Solution to the Jewish Question" – the end of any Jewish presence in Europe and, if the Nazis won the war, the world. Hungary's August 1941 Third Anti-Jewish Law prohibited marriage between Jews and non-Jews.

As Jews from Nazi-occupied countries poured into Hungary and the refugee crisis grew, a few people with the means to be helpful or the ability to obtain funds, food, clothing and living space from others established centres for refugees. One of those people was a small town lawyer and journalist in Kolozsvár in the recently repatriated part of Transylvania. His name was Rezső (Rudolf) Kasztner. Even before 1941 he was already known as a fixer in his home community,

a Jew who could talk with the local authorities and extract imprisoned Jews, provide food and shelter for those escaping persecution,
even intervene in special cases where men were forced into labour
battalions.

In 1941, after the government shut down *Új Kelet*, the Jewish news-
paper where he worked, Kasztner helped set up the Jewish Aid and
Rescue Committee (Va'ada Ezra v'Hazalah) in Budapest. His partners,
Joel and Hansi Brand, had been actively helping refugees in Budapest
ever since the need arose. Their apartment became an aid centre, with
Hansi offering her own clothes to those who arrived with nothing.
Both Kasztner and Brand had evaded labour service with fake medi-
cal certificates. Although the Meisels had no idea until much later,
Rezső Kasztner, along with the Brands, would save their lives.

In August 1941 Hungary deported approximately 20,000 Jews –
many of them refugees without legal papers – to German-controlled
Kamenets-Podolsk in Western Ukraine, where they were massacred
by Einsatzgruppen (mobile killing units).

In January 1942, Hungarian army units executed more than 3,000
civilians in the recently occupied region of Yugoslavia – a third of
those killed were Jews. Early that summer, Rabbi von Freudiger of
the Budapest Orthodox congregation received a letter from Rabbi
Michael Dov Weissmandel in Bratislava telling him that the Germans
had already deported 52,000 Jews from Slovakia and Weissmandel was
working with Gizi Fleischmann of the Women's Zionist Organization
to try to save the rest. The two of them had the idea of bribing the
Germans to save Jewish lives. The Slovak government had agreed to
deport Jews for forced labour to Germany, had paid the Germans
500 reichsmarks per deportee for the exchange; perhaps the Germans
would accept a larger sum to let the Jews remain in their own country.
Weissmandel and Fleischmann had started the process by providing
a down payment of $25,000 received from a local businessman. They
had presented themselves to a Nazi officer called Dieter Wisliceny,
as representatives of a mythical "World Jewry," willing to pay more if

their demands were met. Fleischmann, who referred to their idea as the "Europa Plan" was convinced that in exchange for only $3 million, every remaining Jewish life could be spared.

The group in Bratislava had hoped that the American Jewish Joint Distribution Committee (referred to as the Joint) and the Jewish Agency in Palestine would raise the necessary funds. As it turned out, they couldn't, but both Brand and Kasztner seized on their idea.

During November 1942, more than 300,000 Jews were deported from occupied Europe, including 106,000 from Holland and 27,000 from France. Stephen Wise, president of the American Jewish Congress, announced to a room filled with politicians and journalists that over 2 million Jews had already been killed in Europe and that it was Nazi policy to annihilate them all. The London *Times* reported that 4,000 Jewish children had been transported from Paris to concentration camps. Yet "extermination centres" designed to operate like factories were still impossible to imagine. Jewish leaders in Hungary continued to cling to the idea that the German army would need the railways to transport troops and supplies, not waste it on transporting Jews to camps.

The Hungarians had joined the German offensive against the Soviet Union in June 1941 and, in January 1943, the Second Hungarian Army was virtually destroyed at Voronezh on the Don River. More than half the men were killed, thousands taken prisoner, the labour battalion made up largely of unarmed Jews annihilated. Fortunately for the Meisels family, Lajos Meisels' gentile employer, Alexander Papp, had been able to keep him out of the army, so the Meisels family was not directly affected. In the aftermath of the debacle at Voronezh, however, a chain of events was set in motion that would prove deadly for Hungary's Jews.

In reaction to the heavy losses on the Soviet front, the Hungarian government began to waver with regard to their part in the Axis alliance. When Italy withdrew from the Axis in the fall of 1943, Hungary expressed support for the new Italian regime. The Hungarian government also allowed public criticism on the war in the press, as well as public calls for Hungary to withdraw from the war. The prime minister wrote to Hitler and demanded that Hungary be allowed to call its troops back from the Eastern front. Last but not least, the Hungarian regime refused to round up the country's Jews and deport them to concentration and death camps. Furious, on March 17, 1944, Hitler summoned Regent Horthy to a meeting and raged at the betrayal. He told Horthy that the German army would occupy Hungary and if the Hungarians resisted, he would order all units in the surrounding countries to attack. Making good his threat, on March 19, 1944, the German army rolled into Hungary. The impact on the Jewish community was immediate. At four o'clock on the afternoon of the invasion, two SS officers marched into the offices of the Jewish community organization at 12 Sip Street in Budapest and demanded a meeting with all Jewish leaders – both Orthodox and Neolog – at ten a.m. the next day. One of those officers was Dieter Wisliceny. They demanded the setting up of a Jewish council, as they had done in other countries, to respond to German orders.

The Rescue Committee met the same day to try to figure out how they could help the refugees without papers and fixed addresses who were sure to be among the first ones rounded up when the deportations began. Kasztner and Brand discussed Weissmandel's plan to buy Jewish lives and determined that they would try the same tactic in Hungary.

Lieutenant-Colonel SS Adolf Eichmann arrived in Budapest in late March. His orders, as they had been in other occupied countries, were clear: make Hungary free of Jews. His enthusiastic assistants in this enterprise were State Secretaries Baky and Endre and the chief enforcer was Lieutenant-Colonel Ferenczy of the gendarmerie. As Eichmann recalled in a later interview with a Dutch journalist in Argentina, "On that evening, the fate of the Jews of Hungary was sealed." The country was divided into ghettoization and deportation zones, starting with Carpathian Ruthenia and Transylvania. For Jews, trying to communicate with friends and family in other parts of the country now became impossible as they could no longer travel without written permits, and radios and telephones were forbidden.

By the end of March, all Jews in Hungary were ordered to wear the yellow star on their clothing. Leslie Meisels writes about the traumatic effect of that decree on his paternal grandfather:

This same Hungarian-looking gentleman whose forefathers were born in the town and who had lived respectful lives there, said that he wouldn't be humiliated, he wouldn't wear the yellow star. He brooded about it for two days, not leaving the house. Then, he had a heart attack and passed away a couple of days later. He died without ever putting that symbol on his clothing.

Kasztner and the Va'ada decided they would try to bribe the SS, starting with Wisliceny, but keen to progress to one of the chief mechanics of the Holocaust, Adolf Eichmann. Though the first portion of the down payment was only $90,000 – all gathered from wealthy Jews in the capital – they were optimistic that there would be more from America once they realized that Hungarian Jews were about to be murdered.

When Eichmann summoned Brand to his office in the Buda Hills, the Va'ada members thought they were entering a new phase of bargaining for human lives. But it was not to be. Eichmann's idea was to send Brand to Istanbul to see if the Allies would trade "blood for goods," in this case Jewish lives for winterized trucks. Predictably, Brand's mission failed.

On April 29, the first transport of 1,800 Hungarian Jews left for Auschwitz-Birkenau – the killing grounds for more than a million European Jews. That same month, the Nazis and their Hungarian collaborators began collecting Jews into ghettos at central points of the designated deportation zones.

Having failed to impress Eichmann with the imaginary wealth of "World Jewry," Kasztner determined that his next best bargaining partner would be Lieutenant-Colonel Kurt Becher who had just made a deal with Hungary's wealthiest Jewish family for their lives in exchange for their industrial assets.[3]

On April 30, 1944, Leslie Meisels said goodbye to his father, who was taken into a forced labour battalion, and moved into the Nádudvar ghetto with his mother, his grandmother and his two younger brothers. About two hundred people were crowded into a dozen houses. The entire area was fenced in and guarded by Hungarian gendarmes to make sure no one escaped.

Kasztner continued his negotiations with both Eichmann and SS officer Kurt Becher, promising more funds and valuables, collecting jewellery and silver utensils from those who still had some. In the end, he was able to make a deal to transport 1,684 Jews to Switzerland via Bergen-Belsen in Germany. One hundred of those on the train paid for the rest of the passengers. The price was steep – about 20 million Swiss francs of which a deposit of 5 million was paid.

By the end of May, 217,000 Hungarian Jews had been deported. Gendarmes conducted body searches to find valuables, they beat and tortured people, some of whom died from their wounds. In early June, the Meisels were transferred to a larger ghetto, a former tannery, in Debrecen. Young Meisels was fortunate that his mother was able to get out with the pot of schmaltz (rendered goose fat) that later saved them from starvation. He also managed to secret away his birthday gift of a stamp collection that he still has today. What seventeen-year-old Leslie didn't know is that the transport train he dragged his mother and two brothers on to – against his mother's wishes – saved their lives.

In his negotiations for more lives, Kasztner constantly reminded Eichmann that world Jewry and, indeed, everyone who read the papers, were aware of what was going on in Auschwitz. Two

---

3 The Chorin-Weiss-Kornfeld-Mauthner assets included an aircraft and munitions factory. The family were flown to Spain.

Slovakian Jews, Rudolf Vrba and Alfred Wetzler, had escaped from the Auschwitz-Birkenau death camp on April 7, 1944. Soon after, they wrote a report detailing the process of organized murder that awaited Hungarian Jews once they arrived on the railway ramp at Birkenau. Vrba had witnessed the building of two new crematoria and the ramp itself. The report appeared in the press in Europe and the United States in June and July 1944 – just as the deportations reached their frenzied peak. If no Jews were left alive, Kasztner impressed on Eichmann, bargains for money and equipment would no longer be available.

The first number mentioned was 100,000 Jews, but by June it had dwindled to 30,000, with 100,000 pengos (Hungarian currency), or about $100 per person, on deposit. Eichmann referred to them as "Jews on ice," awaiting further payments from the Joint, the Jewish Agency or whoever in the outside world cared about them.

The Va'ada's instruction was to choose families with a lot of young children. Children under ten, Kasztner expected, were not counted. Given the rush to gather 15,000 from the provinces and 15,000 from Budapest, before it was too late, the responsibility was passed on to what was left of the local Jewish councils. The Vienna office registered 6,889 men and 9,812 women.

Kasztner was unaware that Brigadier-General Karl Blaschke, the mayor of Vienna, had written to ask for relief workers in Austria, as able-bodied Austrians were in the army. That gave the "Jews on ice" another reason to be kept alive. Leslie Meisels' family was among those sent to Strasshof in Austria, while the rest of the 40,500 Jews from Zones IV and V in southern and western Hungary were sent to Auschwitz-Birkenau, where most of them were murdered on arrival.

The Strasshof groups, packed into freight cars without food or water, were sorted into work groups once they arrived in Austria. Many families, like the Meisels, were taken to farms to work the land and gather the crops. Others were kept in Vienna where the small children could be used to clear bombs from hard-to-reach places.

By the end of June, 434,351 Hungarian Jews had been deported to Auschwitz and most of them were dead.

On October 15, Horthy announced in a radio address that Hungary was withdrawing from the war. He and his family were quickly arrested and shipped off to Austria, while a new government of the viciously antisemitic Arrow Cross Party was installed to run the country. By that time, only the Jews of Budapest remained. Thousands were force-marched toward Vienna, ostensibly to build fortifications. Many were shot along the way, while in the city Arrow Cross men invaded houses protected by foreign embassies and shot all the Jews they found, sending them into the Danube dead or alive.

Meanwhile, Becher estimated that the value of Kasztner's original deposit had declined and now there was not enough to pay for the remaining Jews in Strasshof. Kasztner tried to deliver medicines and clothing through the Vienna office, but he realized that many would now be transferred to concentration camps.

In early December, many of the "Jews on ice" – including Leslie Meisels and his family – were sent to Bergen-Belsen's *Ungarnlager* (Hungarian camp), the place that had earlier housed the passengers from the Kasztner train who were waiting to be sent on to Switzerland. The horror that greeted the British 11th Armoured Division on April 15, 1945, when they liberated Bergen-Belsen has been amply documented. The British forced the former guards to bury the mountains of dead.

Before the arrival of the British, the Meisels had been shipped out of the camp and ended up being put on a train with no idea where they were headed. Still on the train – now abandoned by their German guards, they were liberated by the 30th Division of the US Army on April 13, 1945. "After sixty-three years," writes Meisels, "whenever I think about that moment, my skin still shivers."

About the same time that the Meisels were sent to Bergen-Belsen, on December 10, 1944, the Budapest ghetto was surrounded by a sixteen-foot wooden fence. There were 63,000 people crammed into 293 houses with at least fourteen people in each room. Five-year-old Eva Silber, who later became Eva Meisels, was one of them. Her memory of corpses piled in Klauzal Square would haunt her for the rest of her life.

Budapest was taken by the Red Army between January 17 and 18, 1945. After weeks in a basement bomb shelter, little Eva Silber couldn't see in daylight for days and was afraid to go into a basement for most of her childhood. Young as she was, memories of the people taken from her have stayed with her. "There are too many names of our loved ones we lost in the war," she tells us. "This is what I remember. Having a normal life – children and grandchildren – was not what Hitler had in mind for the Jews."

Leslie and Eva Meisels' stories are very different. To a great extent, as is true for most Holocaust survivors, their survival can be attributed to luck or fate. But what both accounts powerfully illustrate is the tremendous difference that one person can make in changing the lives of many. While neither Leslie nor Eva Meisels were aware of the machinations behind the scenes that helped them endure the horrors of the Holocaust, it is almost certain that without the courageous endeavours of Rezső Kasztner and Raoul Wallenberg, their stories would have ended very differently.

Anna Porter
Toronto
2014

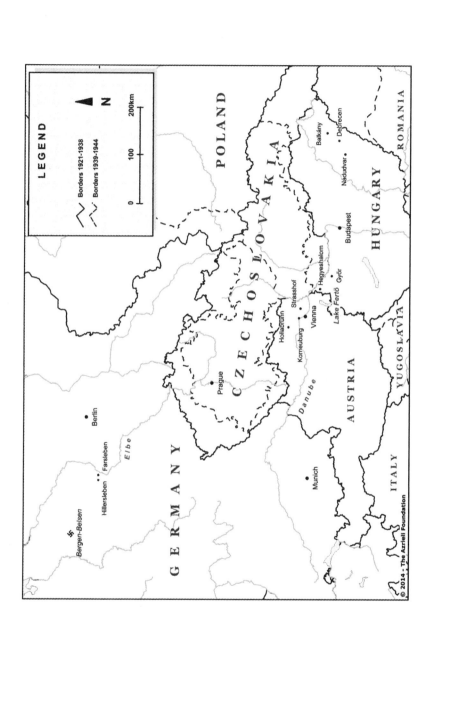

These memoirs were written in honour of our parents, who survived the Holocaust, and in memory of our grandparents and the many aunts, uncles, cousins and other relatives who were murdered by the tyrannical and hateful Nazis.

It is dedicated to our children, their children and future generations. Let the experiences described within the covers of this book be an inspiration for its readers to remember the Holocaust and eradicate hatred. May this keep the memory of the six million victims alive.

Author's Preface

In 1987, after attending a photo exhibit in Toronto on Anne Frank and her family, I contacted someone from the Toronto Holocaust Centre about recording my memoir. Over the next five years, I was so busy that I kept postponing it until a bitter experience made me realize that I should do it while I could: a routine physical had found that there was a tumor growing in my right kidney. I hadn't been ill or had any symptoms. The kidney was removed and with that, the cancer was removed from my body, but it made me realize that we are all mortal. Sooner or later, I will not be able to tell this story and therefore, it is better to do it now.

Between December 1993 and February 1994, Dave Harris from the Holocaust Centre interviewed me at Global Television's facilities and I subsequently augmented my written memoir in the spring of 2007. I volunteered to record my experiences not only to have them on record, but also because every survival story is different. This is my unique experience and maybe others will benefit from my story. I hope that those who read my memoir will be inspired to achieve their life goals and do everything they can to prevent hatred among people. If people can gain some insight into what inhuman atrocities some people are capable of and help prevent them, then writing it has been worthwhile for me.

A Fragile Peace

My childhood was rather idyllic. Our family wasn't rich, but we were comfortable. Mother never worked outside of the home, and she employed a maid to help with the household. When I was born on February 20, 1927, I was the first grandchild on both sides of the family and, for the first six years of my life, I was an only child. My brother György (George), was born on September 10, 1933, and Ferenc (Frank), on September 11, 1934.

My parents were both born in Hungary in the town of Nádudvar, Hajdú county; my father, Lajos Meisels, in 1900 and my mother, Etelka Berkovits, four years later. The Berkovits family had lived in Nádudvar for many years. My maternal grandfather, Morris, owned a general store close to the main market square. On market days, he allowed the peasant women who came to sell their wares from the farms out of town to park their wagons in his yard for free. In turn, the women gave him lists of items they needed to buy from his store, and in this way, his business thrived.

Coincidentally, my father worked in this very store after finishing his Grade 6 education. As a young apprentice, his job was to clean the store after it closed. One night, after he had finished washing the floors, Morris's eight-year-old daughter, Etelka, came in, wanting some candy. My father told her not to step on the floor until it dried but she didn't listen and for this my father spanked her! At the time, he could never have known that this little girl would grow up to become his lifelong, adored wife.

Tragedy struck the Berkovits family in 1916 when my mother's two-year-old sister ran into the street and was struck and killed by a horse. My grandmother never recovered from the shock and died two years later. As a result, my mother became the caretaker of the household at the young age of fourteen and, with the help of the family maid, raised her two brothers, Andor (Andy) and Sandor (Alex), and her sister, Gizella. Perhaps it was this early responsibility that later gave her the strength to help her sons survive the Holocaust.

My father was the sixth generation of Meisels born in Nádudvar, which makes me the seventh, and he told me many stories passed down from his elders about how Jewish life had evolved in our town over several generations. In Hungary, during the Austro-Hungarian Empire, Jews weren't allowed to live or even stay over in large cities like Debrecen, our provincial capital. Debrecen was a *szabad-királyi város*, which means Royal Free City, where Jews were able to work in any kind of occupation or attend to business during the day but they were not allowed to live, sleep or own property there until 1840.[1] The city was of such industrial and commercial importance that, although they had to live elsewhere, many Jews worked there.

My hometown was only forty kilometres from Debrecen and at the turn of the eighteenth century more than two hundred Jewish families lived there, working either in Nádudvar or in Debrecen. Consequently, a large, beautiful synagogue was built in our town, which was seldom done in other similar towns or villages.

After the 1867 emancipation declaration by King and Emperor Franz Josef of the Austro-Hungarian Empire, Jews became equal citizens. From then on they could live, work and own property in any

---

1   For information on Royal Free City, as well as on other historical, religious and cultural terms; major organizations; significant historical events and people; geographical locations; and foreign-language words and expressions contained in the text, please see the glossary.

town or city in the country. Most Jews, from my grandfathers' generation on down, were grateful to have gained equality and began to assimilate into Hungarian culture. People moved away from Nádudvar, many to the big cities. When I was a child, the Jewish community had dwindled to forty-five families out of a population of 10,000.

My paternal grandfather, also named Morris, was born in 1867, the year of emancipation. Raised on a farm where his father was the superintendent, he never went to school or learned to read and write, other than signing his name. However, he had a photographic memory and excellent mathematical skills, which served him well later in life.

Like all young men in Hungary, he was conscripted into the army at age twenty. After serving twelve years, he was released from the military in 1899, when he returned to his hometown, married and established a family.

On that very first summer after his military discharge, my grandfather purchased two horses and a buggy and hired himself out to anyone who needed his services. He got a plum job with a large landowner, hauling wheat sheaves from the harvested fields to the threshing machine. The work started at 3:00 a.m. and paused for a communal breakfast around 7:00 a.m. One morning, the boss honoured my grandfather by asking him to do the blessing and cut the bread for the group, knowing and accepting that he would do this *motzi*, the blessing, in Hebrew. When the maid gave the large, round, seven-kilogram bread to my grandfather, he asked the boss where he wanted him to cut it and the boss responded, "Wherever you want to, Morris." My grandfather answered, "At home," so the boss told the servant girl to put that one aside for him to take home and bring another one for breakfast. That loaf of bread lasted the family for a whole week!

Following the outbreak of World War I, my grandfather was called back into the military and it fell upon my grandmother and father to support the family, which now included his two younger brothers, Eugene (called Jeno) and Istvan (Steven), as well as his youngest sibling, his sister, Etus (Eta). Grandmother raised and fattened geese in the backyard to harvest goose liver and my father, at age fifteen, then made a weekly 215-kilometre trip by train to Budapest to sell it. In 1917, my father, too, was drafted into the army. Unlike my grandfather, he had gone to school for the compulsory six grades and had beautiful, legible handwriting, so he was selected to serve as a scribe for a platoon. Because of this, my father never saw the front lines during World War I.

After the war, both my grandfather and my father returned home. My grandfather expanded his business with the assistance of two partners and became a livestock dealer. His inability to read and write never interfered with his success. My father worked with my grandfather for a number of years and also became very knowledgeable in livestock, so much so that he later secured a contract from the military to purchase cattle for butchering and horses for the Hussar (cavalry) divisions of the army in our district. This experience provided him with the necessary expertise to open his own kosher butcher shop with his brother Jeno just before he married my mother.

$\sim$

When I was three years old, both sets of grandparents decided to buy me a special gift. Grandfather Meisels purchased a donkey foal and Grandfather Berkovits ordered a small wagon and a special harness for the donkey from a local tradesman. I remember riding up and down the street in the wagon, pulled by the donkey, with my father's employee running alongside.

I may have been a bit spoiled as a child, and I was strong-willed, too. When I turned four, my mother decided that I should attend the nursery school close to our home. I got up in the morning, dressed in my best clothes, and the maid walked me to school. When I returned home at the end of the day I told my mother that one day was enough, I wasn't going back. And I never did.

My childhood felt normal, unmarked by special events, although being Jewish meant certain differences. While my neighbour's children were spending their time in whatever way they wanted, from the age of five I attended cheder, or religious studies, several times a week to learn about being Jewish, about our history and how to daven (pray). At cheder, the *melamed* (teacher) was also one of the community's *shochetim*, a ritual slaughterer; the teacher taught us to read Hebrew and explained, in Hungarian, the basics of the five books of Moses.

When I turned six, I attended public school, as did other Jewish children, because with so few of us, there was no Jewish school. There were two parochial schools, one Protestant and one Roman Catholic, and in those days, public school consisted of either four grades, which led to junior high, or six. If children graduated with relatively good grades and their parents were able to pay for higher education, they went on to junior high school for another four years.

In such a small town, everybody knew all the Jewish people, every Jew knew every other Jew, and all the Jewish people knew, if not by name, by face, most of the people in town. When I was growing up, we identified ourselves as patriotic Hungarians who practised the Jewish religion. I felt like our Jewish community was entirely integrated, accepted and respected in town. However, there were times that I was on my way to or from school when a child, who might have been angry with me, called me a "dirty Jew." It was unpleasant, but it didn't go any further than that.

Life changed radically for my family in 1934. My father lost his business because of the Great Depression and was forced to look for some other way to provide for our family. He decided to purchase a small hand and household soap manufacturing business in the town of Balkány, about forty kilometres northeast of Debrecen. He bought all the ingredients to make the soap, cooked, dried, cut and stamped it, and then drove his horse and buggy to the surrounding towns to sell to merchants.

We moved to Balkány in 1935 when I was in Grade 2 and we lived there until 1939. During those four years, we became part of a much larger Jewish community of one hundred or so families in a town of only six thousand. I attended a Hebrew school where I spent half a day in secular studies in one room and then transferred to another room for the afternoon's study of religion, including davening, Chumash (the five books of the Torah), and works by the Jewish scholar Rashi. I didn't progress much farther because I didn't come from an ultra-Orthodox family but an assimilated Orthodox one; we observed the religious rules, kept kosher and went to synagogue every Friday night, Saturday and holidays. While my grandparents on both sides understood Yiddish, my parents and my brothers and I did not. We only spoke our mother tongue: Hungarian.

Our life in Balkány was similar to the way we had lived in Nádudvar: our neighbours were both Jews and gentiles who knew that we were Jewish and accepted us as we accepted them. I sometimes still experienced the "dirty Jew" type of comment, which could happen for no reason at all.

At the end of 1938, the economic situation worsened for small tradespeople and my father's business was threatened and eventually destroyed by a large company that used modern equipment to mass produce much nicer-looking soap. The soap wasn't actually better, but this mass production forced out all the smaller businesses. When my father's business faltered to the point that he was unable to support us, he had to once again look for another way to earn a living. Since my father and his preceding generations were born and brought up in Nádudvar, my parents ultimately decided that the best thing would be to move back and find some kind of livelihood in a place where he knew everyone and everyone knew him.

I was twelve years old and finishing the compulsory Grade 6 because my parents couldn't afford to send me to junior high after Grade 4, and they waited until the end of the school year to move back. In Nádudvar, my father found work right away and made plans to send me to junior high school even though it meant I'd have to travel twenty kilometres to the one in the nearby town of Hajdúszoboszló. The junior high school there would admit me in the third year if I successfully completed an equivalency test. To prepare for it, my father hired a teacher to tutor me for six or eight weeks during the summer.

My father's new position was a relatively well-paid, responsible job for Alexander Papp, whose father, also named Alexander, was a landowner of more than one thousand hectares. To put that in perspective, owning just fifteen hectares provided a good living for a small farmer. Prior to my father's birth, the elder Papp became acquainted with my paternal grandfather and made him his agent. My grandfather oversaw the sale and purchase of wheat, other crops and livestock that were raised on the estate and was also in charge of replenishing the stock of special horses that had to be absolutely perfect for Mr. Papp's personal carriage. As Mr. Papp aged, his son, who happened to be within a year of my father's age, took over and my father almost automatically became his trusted agent. Since my father was a butcher, he knew a lot about raising and fattening livestock.

Alexander Papp liked my father, which was one of the reasons we had come back to Nádudvar. At the end of the summer of 1939, Mr. Papp bought the bigger of the two existing flour mills in town on condition that my father take one of the most important and trustworthy positions in the organization. The Tiszavideki Hengermalom, the Tisza River Area Flour Mill, had the capacity not only to grind wheat for local consumption, as the other mill did, but also – importantly – to produce flour for commercial and military purposes. My father accepted the position and became head of the wheat receiving department, which both weighed the wheat and judged its quality, assigning the proper value for it. There was first, second and third-grade flour, the latter being used for fattening hogs, and the mill's payment was a certain percentage of the ground flour. People also brought in their own wheat that they had either grown or earned during the course of the year. Landless peasants, for example, were paid for their work in hundreds of kilograms of wheat, corn or livestock and then sold these commodities to buy other necessities. To get flour, the basic staple for baking, they took their own wheat to the mill.

The flour mill's success depended on the honesty and integrity of the department my father ran and he had about a dozen people working under him. He made a very different living from before – the job didn't make him rich but it paid well enough and it turned out to be life-saving.

This point in 1939 was one year after the first anti-Jewish law that the Hungarian fascist government, which politically supported the German Nazi regime, had independently implemented. The law restricted the number of Jews who could participate in businesses and commercial enterprises. In spite of this, my family and I were not yet experiencing any major changes, but on May 5, 1939, the government issued a second, more severe anti-Jewish law that further restricted the number of Jews in certain professions, restricted admission to higher education and forbid Jews from operating large businesses. They could only continue working if they officially transferred management of their businesses to non-Jews. Although Jewish businesses and tradespeople in Nádudvar suffered from these laws, many had trustworthy gentile friends and acquaintances who allowed their names to be used for the government requirements, sometimes for a fee, allowing the Jewish owners to continue managing their own businesses.

That same year, government-organized anti-Jewish propaganda suddenly started to appear everywhere. Although we were afraid to a certain extent, we still thought that nothing worse than the curtailing laws would happen to us. We considered ourselves to be patriotic Hungarians first and Jews second, and native Hungarians were emphatic that these laws were not aimed at us, the central Hungarian Jewish population who had been Hungarian citizens for generations, but rather at Jews in the north and east who were not "originally" Hungarian. As painful as it was to hear this, we were hoping that it was true. Soon enough, though, we found out that our beliefs were just sweet dreams. In the regime's eyes, not only were we not Hungarians, our lives were not worth anything.

The atmosphere in Nádudvar began to change. A man by the last name of Zana, the town electrician, was also the local leader of the Nyilas, the Arrow Cross party, which was the Hungarian version of the German Nazi party. The Arrow Cross had adopted Nazi beliefs, although in its early days its followers only verbally abused Jews in confrontations on the street; their actions didn't go any further until much later. It turned out that the tutor my father had hired to help me pass the equivalency test, who had grown up with him and was very knowledgeable and well respected, was a friend and follower of Zana and the Arrow Cross. He openly expressed his antisemitism but was still willing to help me prepare for the test for a fee. He was actually quite nice to me – strict, but nice. I had heard quite a few comments about him being an antisemite, and I don't think that by agreeing to tutor me he changed his mind about Jews, but he was a childhood friend of my father's and I was my father's son so he must have simply put those feelings aside.

My teacher, who had been a lieutenant in the Hungarian army, was called up for military service just before the test. In pre-war Hungary, every person of military age, which meant from eighteen to forty-five, was in the reserve as a common soldier or officer and was called up for three months of military exercises every year. We didn't know it then, but the government was planning a new, different kind of labour service for Jews.

When my tutor was called up, I had to finish preparing for the test alone. I passed and was accepted to the third year in the Hajdúszoboszló junior high school. Each day, I had to take the train to a small town called Kaba and then change trains and walk two and a half kilometres from the railway station to the school. I did this in good or bad weather for five and a half days of the week.

According to the rules of Shabbat, the Sabbath, I couldn't take the train to school on Saturdays, but the school required me to either take lodgings in Hajdúszoboszló, which we couldn't afford, or break that religious law and travel. Jewish students were exempted from writing and working in the school's garden on that day, which prompted several negative remarks from other classmates who had to dig in the dirt while the Jewish students stood around holding the spades or hoes. When the raspberries were ripening, the few of us placated some of our classmates by picking raspberries for them while they were digging.

~

My father was called up for military service just a few months after my bar mitzvah, in the summer of 1940. It so happened that he was taken to his regular military unit even though Jews were not generally included in regular military service then. He was forty years old and took part in the operation to seize Northern Transylvania from Romania. The area comprised approximately 40 per cent of Transylvania, which the Axis powers of Germany and Italy awarded to Hungary as a reward for its alliance. Fortunately, this military manoeuvre was carried out fairly peacefully. Romania had no choice but to cede the territory and moved out when the Hungarian military took over. We didn't know how long my father would be gone, but less than a month later, he was released from military service, came home and continued to work in the flour mill.

Some Jews hadn't been demobilized but instead were forced to work in labour camps. The following year, in April 1941, the fascist Hungarian government enacted a new law that required military-age Jewish soldiers to report to specially formed forced labour units. They had no rank and no right to weapons aside from a spade and shovel, which became the symbols of this force. Jews in the forced labour battalions were eventually sent to the Eastern front to dig trenches, maintain roads and do the horrendous work of clearing minefields. Minesweepers didn't exist then, so the Hungarian army officers herded these unfortunate people in front of their units to be blown up, clearing a path for them. The platoon commanders and low-ranking soldiers who volunteered to supervise and guard these forced labourers were, for the most part, openly antisemitic followers of the Arrow Cross party. Some were sadistic and enjoyed making life miserable for the Jews under them, sometimes cruelly beating them and telling them that they would never be going back to their homes and families.

In June 1941, Hungary joined in Germany's newly declared war against the Soviet Union. Military exercises had been going on in the country for three years; the land near my hometown, where the boundary extended into the Hortobágy, the Hungarian *puszta*, or Great Plain, was used for that purpose annually. That year, the government ruled that during military exercises in the surrounding towns the "untrustworthy" Jewish people weren't allowed to travel freely – we could only travel if we had special passes.

My grandfather, a fifth-generation Meisels in Nádudvar, was seventy-four at this time and still a very good-looking gentleman who sported a big Hungarian-style moustache. He was an honest, hard-working man who looked, behaved and lived like any small businessman, and had lived there except for his twelve years of compulsory military service in the Austro-Hungarian army. Both Jews and non-Jews liked him and respected him. My grandfather was also an honorary member of the small landowners' club and on Sunday mornings, after its members came out of church, he sat on benches with them, talking and passing the time.

In July 1941, my grandfather decided that since it was a nice summer day, he would go by horse and buggy to visit his youngest son, Steven, my father's younger brother, who lived in Karcag, about twenty-five kilometres away from us. Because it had rained the day before, the straightforward route along an unpaved road would have been difficult, so he decided to take the paved roads as far as Püspökladány, the city in between Nádudvar and Karcag. As I was his oldest grandson, he always took me with him when I was not in school and on that day he asked me to go with him. "What about the travel permit?" I asked. "Oh, don't worry about that," he replied. He said that they wouldn't have given it to him anyway, just for wanting to see his son. So we left without trying to get one. When we were stopped at a military checkpoint, the soldier manning the stop saluted and said, "Sir, if everybody looked like you, like a real Hungarian, then we wouldn't have to have this checkpoint. Please proceed." We were barely able to suppress our smiles.

~

During this time, I finished junior high school. I could only dream of going to high school, impossible for me now because of the restrictions against Jews in Hungary. Had I been from a wealthy family or exceptionally talented, I might have been able to enter school with a scholarship or get into a profession by means of my parents' money; since I was just an average kid – and Jewish – higher education for a professional future was out of the question. Instead, I had to learn a trade. I had to apprentice first and then become what was called a journeyman, later a master, and make my living that way.

From the available trades in town, I chose cabinetmaking and signed a contract with a master by the name of Morris Straussman, who was also Jewish. I started my three-year apprenticeship in September 1941. Mr. Straussman employed four journeymen and four apprentices and had a new apprentice every year; that fall, I was the youngest apprentice in his shop. I began to learn to work with wood, producing fine, custom-made furniture. Everything was handmade, hand-sawn and hand-planed because we didn't have any kind of machinery to do the work. I would have finished my apprenticeship at the end of August 1944 if the Holocaust had not altered my life plan.

Throughout this time, my father was continually called up to report for the forced labour service, but every year Mr. Papp signed a paper saying that since the flour mill was supplying the military, his enterprise and its employees should be exempted. His plea was accepted. However, the Axis powers were increasingly being defeated on the Eastern front and as their situation worsened, more and more people were called up, no matter the circumstances. Jews couldn't avoid the service and continue to work, as they had before. In early 1943, when my father had to report to his base, the document from Mr. Papp wasn't enough. Hearing this, Mr. Papp jumped into his car, drove to my father's base and arranged his release again, this time with an interesting twist. A first cousin of my father's had been ordered to report to the same base on the same day and Mr. Papp, not knowing that there was another Meisels there, didn't mention a first name to the commandant. After Mr. Papp drove away, the commandant realized that he didn't know which Meisels they had been talking about, so he released both of them. Because of this, my father's first cousin Paul, Pal in Hungarian, also survived the Holocaust. He passed away at age seventy-eight in Stockholm, Sweden.

At the end of 1943, Mr. Papp was no longer allowed to employ Jews and he had to let my father go. That winter, our family survived by doing work that the municipality organized for the unemployed. We had to weave overshoes out of a certain kind of bulrush for Hungarian and German soldiers who used them to protect their feet from freezing in the harsh Russian winter. The pay was minimal but at least Jews were allowed to participate. My parents, my younger brothers and I helped when school or work permitted. A short time later, my father got another job from the municipality hauling stones from the railway station for road repair. This was extremely hard work but paid well enough to keep a pair of horses with enough left over for the family to live on.

I had been attending apprenticeship training school along with thirty to forty apprentices from other trades one night a week. We were learning business skills like basic accounting that we would need to become a journeyman and, eventually, a master. I was scared of one of my classmates, a butcher's apprentice by the name of Molnar. He was about two years older than me, six foot five and more than two hundred pounds, and a member of the Arrow Cross Party. Although he didn't pay too much attention to me, he made it clear, often and vehemently, that he didn't like Jews. I avoided stepping in front of him or provoking him, worried about being beaten up. One wintry Friday night, however, he decided to show off, saying, "Hey guys, take a look. I'm going to scare the shit out of this Jewish boy." And as soon as these words were said, his butcher knife flew through the air and stuck into the top of my desk, vibrating, just inches away from my chest and face. He didn't beat me up, but it scared me enough to want to stay as far away from him as possible.

Molnar was amused and some of my classmates laughed, cheered and clapped. Others kept quiet and some expressed their disapproval and support for me by looks and later on by words, but they certainly didn't do anything to stop him. The atmosphere in class was much divided – like the rest of Hungarian society – between verbal anti-semites, sympathizers who didn't act on their beliefs, and the majority, who just remained silent. People let Jews be antagonized as long as they themselves were left alone.

About a month or two after this knife-throwing incident, I was on my way home from school around 7:00 p.m., walking with a dozen or so people. My home was just ten or twelve houses away from the school and I was halfway there when one young boy said, "Hey, how about having a little fun with the Jew-boy. Let's throw him in the snow." There were ditches for spring water flow all along the sidewalk that were now full of snow, and they threw me in, piling snow on top of me. I don't think that they intended serious harm; they were having fun at my expense and later would laugh at the story about how they buried the Jewish boy in the snow. Luckily one of the chimney-sweep apprentices, Steve, was a good-hearted boy who took it a little differently from the others. He ran to my house and called for my father, explaining what was going on. When they came to my rescue, the other boys took off for home. By the time my father pulled me out, my mouth, nose and ears were blocked with snow. Steve had helped save me – another few minutes and I might have suffocated.

These were little incidents that occurred just because I was Jewish, but that winter, the butcher's apprentice was part of something more deadly. One evening, when my old teacher from cheder was going home from the grocery store after work, carrying a bag of potatoes, he encountered Molnar, who stabbed him in the back with his butcher knife, killing him. His excuse was that a Jew was gathering food at night, taking it away from the gentile population.

When the gendarmes took him in, there was no question that he had committed a crime – he didn't deny it and there were witnesses – but he had *only killed a Jew*. Although there must have been a trial, he wasn't imprisoned. He may have received a warning but continued living in town as if nothing had happened. This was the first drastic act that my hometown experienced and it created terrible feelings within the entire community. I'm sure that it even touched the non-Jewish population, especially those who didn't mean harm but didn't dare to speak out, fearing they would be hurt, too. Our small Jewish community was shaken and afraid, not knowing who could be next.

Surrounded by Silence

The German army occupied Hungary on March 19, 1944. Within weeks, they decreed that Jewish people put a cloth yellow Star of David on their garments, which had to be visible so that everybody could see that we were Jews.

My paternal grandfather, sadly, experienced this degradation. This same Hungarian-looking gentleman whose forefathers were born in the town and who had lived respectful lives there, said that he wouldn't be humiliated, he wouldn't wear the yellow star. He brooded about it for two days, not leaving the house. Then, he had a heart attack and passed away a couple of days later. He died without ever putting that symbol on his clothing. We were permitted to have a funeral; in April 1944 he was the last person buried in the Jewish cemetery of Nádudvar. After the war, my father erected a concrete cover on his grave that couldn't be removed or destroyed. It was a good thing that he did because even today, with no Jews living in town, the grave is untouched. My grandfather's death was our immediate family's first real tragedy from the Nazi occupation.

Although at the beginning of the Nazi occupation we could continue working and moving about in town, my employer and his wife decided to prepare for any eventuality by stockpiling some basic staples. Like many Jews, they used schmaltz, or goose fat, for everything – on bread, and for cooking and baking. When mixed with flour, schmaltz becomes a thickening for gravy and sauces; mixed with roasted flour it can be used to make any kind of cooked food. One day my master asked me, his only Jewish employee, to stay after work and help him bury a large container of goose fat in the woodshed. We dug a hole and then covered it with boards so that it was unnoticeable. He was sure it looked fine and he knew that I wouldn't tell anybody.

A few days later, however, an apprentice named Balazs must have somehow noticed that there was fresh dirt in the woodshed – either that or he had stayed behind and spied on us – and he turned us in. Although his father had grown up with my father, had served in the military with him and was a good friend to my father and to the Jewish people in general, his own son was a member of the Arrow Cross party. That Friday night when I was going home from work, as I passed the City Hall, a gendarme came out of nearby headquarters and brought me into the station. They sat me down and told me exactly what criminal act I had committed by burying that staple food in the woodshed, saying that I deserved whatever punishment I got. The Hungarian government, even before the anti-Jewish laws came into effect, was such a strong police-state regime that if someone was caught stealing a chicken, they were so badly beaten that it could take them months or years to recover. Now, as antisemitism took a greater hold on the country, Jews who did anything to break the rules were not only beaten but might be taken away, who knew where. Mr. Straussman had to pay a heavy fine, but he could afford it. Perhaps no harm came to him because he was over sixty years old and a much-respected tradesman.

Fortunately for me, a decent man who worked at the station saw my arrest and went to our home to tell my father that I was being held. My father ran to Mr. Alexander Papp's house to ask for his help and, on learning that he was playing cards at the gentlemen's club with the major and the German commandant, ran to the club. There, he asked the attendant to tell Mr. Papp that Lajos Meisels needed to see him urgently. He came out immediately and after my father explained the situation to him, I was out, free and unharmed, within ten minutes. Mr. Papp may have given me back my life.

Near the end of April 1944, my father was instructed to report for forced labour on May 1; this time, he had no way of escaping. At this same time, all the Jews of Nádudvar were ordered to abandon our homes, take whatever we could and move into a ghetto. All young gentile men born before December 31, 1926, were called up for military service and all Jews born before that date were ordered to report for forced labour. Since I was born in February 1927, those two months saved me and made it possible for me to stay with the rest of my family in the ghetto.

My father still owned a buggy and two horses, so carrying out his plan for moving our belongings, as well as those of some other families, into the ghetto became my job when he had to report to a forced labour camp. According to the rail schedule, my father would have to leave Nádudvar at around noon on April 30 or, if he could be at Kaba, ten kilometres away on the main rail line, at 5:00 a.m. on May 1. So that he could have some extra time with us, I took him to the Kaba station, where I said a sad and bewildered goodbye to him. I had only seen my father cry once before, at his own father's death. Now, he wept and hugged me tightly. He said, "I do not know what is going to happen; take care of yourself, your mother and your brothers. Don't forget your grandmother."

When I got back to Nádudvar, I started to move everything into the ghetto, which was comprised of one or two dozen fenced-in houses around the synagogue. Jews from the smaller communities of Kaba, Földes and Tetétlen were also brought there, so between 200 and 250 people were crowded into this small enclosure. The four of us, plus my widowed grandmother, shared a standard-sized bedroom with two other families. It was extremely crammed but bearable.

Aside from the crowding living quarters and the fact that we were treated like prisoners – the only gate was guarded by gendarmes around the clock – life in the ghetto went on with relative normalcy. As a strong young boy who owned a pair of horses and a buggy, I was given the daily chore of taking garbage out and bringing basic supplies into the ghetto. Not having to constantly be in the prison-like atmosphere of the ghetto was an advantage, and on occasion, a townsperson who was not a Nazi sympathizer risked arrest and who knows what else by asking me to smuggle a small package to a friend or neighbour inside the ghetto. Sometimes that little package was directed to my own family. I was in contact with good, decent, Christian Hungarians who were sorry to see our plight and helped by giving me bread, potatoes or beans, which I smuggled in with other goods. I wasn't searched all that thoroughly and the guards could have found the contraband if they wanted to, but they didn't care that much. The local gendarmerie guarding the ghetto in my hometown was, for the most part, better than the guards in many other places I heard about. They weren't all that cruel, even though they were taking part in a system that forced us to abandon our homes and live a restricted life with restricted goods.

After about a month in the ghetto, on one of the first days of June 1944, everyone was assembled in the synagogue square, where the gendarmes put down a blanket and ordered us all to throw our valuables such as jewellery and watches onto it. Our only gold jewellery was my mother's wedding band. We were a little farther back in the line and my mother whispered to me, "They won't get this one." She told me to pretend that I had to go to the outhouse and to drop it in there, which I did. Even today, I feel smug about that one piece of jewellery that they did not put into their own pockets.

After giving up our valuables we were told to put whatever we could carry into suitcases or pillowcases – we would be moving on and that was all that we were allowed to take. I packed my stamp collection, which I had had since I was eight years old; the stamps were a pretty good variety from around the world, and my aunt had given me an album for them for my ninth birthday. The collection wasn't valuable, but as I grew up it enhanced my knowledge of geography, the currency of different countries and historical personalities and places. Looking after my collection also taught me skills in sorting and organizing. It was, and is, a good hobby that has stayed with me for life. My mother hurriedly packed a few items of clothing, family photographs and some basic food supplies. She also took a pot full of schmaltz, carrying it in one of the pillowcases that held our belongings.

At the end of the day, when we were marched from the ghetto to the railway station, I was unprepared for what I experienced out on the main street. It was lined with people, several dozen of whom were members of the Arrow Cross and were laughing and clapping loudly, showing their happiness that the Jews were being taken away and yelling insulting, derogatory remarks. Perhaps they were already thinking how wonderful it would be the next morning to loot our abandoned houses. Behind them, hundreds of people stood silently, which was painfully disturbing. Up until then, I had thought better of most people in my hometown.

In central Hungary, there was no uprising against the Nazis or their collaborators, not like there was in Slovakia or Poland. Since the beginning of the 1920s, Hungarian society had been homogeneous, a regulated police state, and people probably didn't dare to risk the wrath of those loudmouth antisemites. Even with that in mind, this behaviour was still a blow to us; their silence was a shock that has stayed with me all my life.

The next morning, we arrived in Debrecen, where the gendarmes were concentrating the Jewish people from the smaller ghettos before deporting them somewhere else by train. These larger ghettos were brickyards or similar establishments on the edges of the city; we were put into a hide-processing plant, a tannery that was worse than a brickyard would have been. Because the hides were processed by soaking them in bins of water until the hair fell off, the place had only outer walls; it didn't have a roof because rain or snow was a welcome addition to the processing operation. For the Germans and their Hungarian associates, it was a good enough place to keep us in.

I cannot recall how many roofless buildings there were, but between three and five thousand people had been amassed. The one we were forced to stay in was so crowded that the five of us were only able to put down our belongings. At night, my grandmother and my little brothers crouched down on them, trying to sleep. My mother and I had to stand, planting our feet among them, leaning against each other to try and sleep or nap, whatever we could manage. On top of this inhumane compression, it started to rain on the first night and continued to rain steadily for two days and nights. We stood in mud, soaked to the skin.

In the daytime, we were permitted to roam within the enclosed area. I saw terribly sadistic gendarmes, strangers who had been brought in from other parts of the country to eliminate the possibility of leniency toward people they might know. They beat people, punishing them for even the slightest infraction. On the first day I saw one of the oldest people from my town, Louis Angyal, who was very hard of hearing, feeble and near-blind, walking with a white cane in the middle of the yard where freight cars stood with open doors. While he shuffled around in the yard, a guard yelled at him to stop, but since he didn't hear, he kept walking. After the third yell, they grabbed him, beat him and hung him up by his wrists from the corners of one of the freight car's doors. He lost consciousness within minutes and they didn't even take him down. They left him there to show others what would happen to those who didn't obey orders. They did this only because we were Jews.

On the third day, there was an announcement that families with five or more children had to report to the railway track, where a group was being assembled for transport. We knew that people were being taken away, but the government's propaganda emphasized that any rumours we heard about Jews undergoing cruelty at the hands of the Nazis was just that, a rumour; they made us believe that for the remainder of the war, which we hoped would be short, we were being sent somewhere for slave labour. As bad as that seemed, we still thought that if they wanted our labour, they would have to give us food and shelter. At the tannery we had nothing, and we believed that anywhere else would be better. We didn't know at that time about the Nazis' unparalleled, unimaginable annihilation plan, already working full blast in Auschwitz and the other death camps.

Later, there was another announcement calling for families with four children to report to the train. One of my best friends, who had four siblings and was going to be on that transport, came to me saying that they had heard that they needed eight more families with three children to make up the quota and asked if we wanted to come along with their group. I went back to my mother and told her this, even though nobody knew where the people on the transport were going or what would happen to the rest of us. My mother said we shouldn't go because they hadn't called for families with three children.

I have to explain that in those days, a seventeen-year-old never, ever said no to his or her parents. Up to that moment, I, too, had never spoken back to my mother, but this time I said, "We're not staying! We're going!" We argued back and forth until I grabbed my belongings and started to walk. She had no choice but to follow. My father had already been taken away to the unknown and she didn't want her family to be broken up any further. I didn't know then, and I still don't know now, what made me defy my mother, but it was the first miracle of my survival.

Starting mid-morning, we were ordered to march through the outskirts of Debrecen and about fifteen kilometres later our group arrived at an estate outside of the city called Jozsa-Puszta. There, we were sent into a huge tobacco shed where straw and blankets had been laid down next to the walls for us to put down our belongings. A communal kitchen had been set up and we were given some soup and other basic food; the conditions were relatively comfortable compared to those in the tannery. We didn't have to wait too long before we received the next order to move – a few days later we were told to gather our belongings and were marched half a kilometre to the railway track where a train with freight wagons stood.

These freight cars were small, and with just over one hundred people forced into the space, we reverted back to a state that was the same as, or even more dreadful than, what we had experienced in the tannery. Some of us were able to sit down, but there wasn't enough room to lie down. My family managed to secure a little space for ourselves in a corner where we could sleep sitting or leaning against each other.

The doors closed and the train took off to an unknown destination. In that closed-in, dark, crowded place we were given two twenty-five-litre pails, one with drinking water and one for human waste. The water was soon gone and the waste pail flowed over. These were changed, refilled and emptied once a day when we stopped at a station.

We were able to see through the small, barbed-wired window above our little corner and knew from the stations that we were heading toward Budapest. I think I passed it on the second day; that night, the last station I saw through the window was Kassa, or Košice, Slovakia. Surprisingly, the first station the next morning was again Kassa and then, later on, Budapest. Soon we passed Győr in western Hungary and on the seventh day we arrived at a town called Strasshof in Austria. During those seven days, my mother gave each of us a few spoonfuls of roasted flour and by the time we arrived in Strasshof, we had consumed about half of the pot.

Strasshof, about twenty-five kilometres northeast of Vienna, was a central transit station for deportees arriving from Hungary and other places. When the door opened, we heard Germans harshly yelling, "Raus! Raus!" (Out! Out!) As we left our car, I saw several bodies being carried out from each of the wagons. Six or eight bodies were carried out of ours. Many had succumbed from lack of food, water and ventilation.

We were all sent into a large room and together – children, adolescent boys and girls, mothers, grandmothers and grandfathers – had to disrobe and march naked to a shower between two lines of laughing, pointing, machine-gun-toting SS guards with dogs. Walking to that shower was the very first real dehumanization I experienced. It drove into our minds the fact that we were not who we used to be, not individuals who had our own dignity, respected within our communities, but, rather, people who the SS guards considered to be sub-human. I was stunned, as were my mother and grandmother.

All those laws that had existed in Hungary for a number of years and prevented Jews from living a free and normal life, even the German occupation and being forced to wear the yellow star – none of it was as psychologically damaging as this was. It wasn't just a physically and mentally unpleasant experience – this was the ultimate shock from which I don't think I recovered until my final liberation and the realization that I had survived. This was something a person cannot ever forget.

A Brief Respite

After the shower we were given back our clothes and told to wait outside, where we'd soon be sent somewhere to work. Compared to the previous weeks' experiences, this was a relief. Our group consisted of twenty-one people from four family remnants – "remnants" because almost all of our fathers had been taken away to the forced labour service. We were with the Bleiers, a widow with four children from my hometown, Mrs. Bleier's sister-in-law with her three children from the nearby town of Püspökladány, and the Leib family of seven from Kaba. Mr. Leib, who was above military age, was the only man to remain with his family.

As we waited, we saw some of the people who had come with us on the train being led back to the cattle wagons and we all wondered where they were going. When we saw that our respected rabbi, Yisrael Jungreis, and his wife, the rebbetzin, who were both in their late seventies, were being forced into one of these cattle wagons, my mother gave me the half-full pot of roasted flour and told me to take it to them because they might need it. I went right over to the wagon where the rebbetzin and rabbi were and, finding the door slightly open, gave them the pot from my mother. After thanking me, the rabbi put his hands on top of my head and recited the priestly blessing, "May God keep you…bless you and be gracious to you…." It was very moving and I felt touched. He had barely finished the blessing when an SS guard came over and slammed the door shut, pushing me away. This has always stayed with me.

Shortly after I returned to my family, a man came over and introduced himself as the representative of a landowner from a nearby farm. He told us that we would all be going with him. I didn't know the landowner's name at the time but I recently learned from someone else in our group that it was Siegfried Sandler, and that he was the biggest landowner in town. We were driven about sixty kilometres north of Strasshof to a farm outside of a little town called Hollabrunn, where we were led to a small house that had one large room, a kitchen and a very small storage room. In the large room, which would serve as our sleeping quarters, there were two rows of blankets and straw put down for bedding. The widow and her four children took the storage room, her sister-in-law and her three children took the short row of makeshift beds and my family and the Leibs took the longer row. We had only the straw and blankets, no other furniture, but it was heaven compared to where we had just come from.

Of the twenty-one people, there were six who weren't required to work – the five children under twelve years and my grandmother, who was sixty-six. Someone from the farm told us that one person should remain behind as cook and provide all the meals for the entire group. The children would carry lunch, the main meal of the day, to the rest of us wherever we were working.

The person who gave us orders turned out to be the farm's foreman. He had authority over two other slave labour groups of about the same size; one group was made up of Soviet POWs and the other of Ukrainian women. The foreman was relatively nice, though stern, and he stressed that we would have to work from dawn to dusk six days a week and that we weren't to go anywhere else. We would have Sundays off and would not be guarded as long as we stayed at the farmhouse. He also said that if we worked hard, we'd be supplied with enough food.

The group nominated my mother as the cook and she immediately began to prepare supper from the available food. The foreman told me and the oldest boy from the Leib family, who was also seventeen, to go with him. We would be working with two German-language-oriented oxen, so we would need to become fluent in German. I had learned the language in junior high because it was compulsory and I improved my fluency over our time there. We managed to harness the oxen to the wagon and lead them to where the vegetables were stored so that we could load up the wagon with as many potatoes, beans and corn as we needed.

We were allowed to eat as much as we wanted and it kept us in good shape, so we were able to work to their satisfaction. Fortunately for us, there were fruit trees – cherry, apple, pear and plum – growing around the farmhouse and we could pick as much of the ripening fruit as we wanted. When the children came back from delivering our lunch, they, along with my mother, gathered as much fruit as they could. My brothers coped with this new reality, and aside from their minor chores, they mostly played. My mother used the fruit they collected for cooking, making soups and compotes. What she didn't use for cooking, she laid out to dry. She had no idea if we would be working at the farm until the end of the war – and, if not, who knew where we'd end up – so she put that dried fruit away for wintertime or for whatever might come.

The farm work, which at first involved hoeing the different crops, turned out to be quite gruelling but we were provided with plenty of food and our bosses, I have to admit, were quite decent – while we worked as slave labourers we received the same bread, sugar and meat rations as the Austrian population. It wasn't much, just the basic necessities, but we felt that it showed that even though we weren't free, we were being treated as almost equal human beings again.

We had to be ready to go to work every morning at dawn. If the field was close by then we walked and if it was far we were taken by truck. Many days at lunchtime we knew without watches what time it was because the Allied forces flew overhead, bringing their "presents" – their bombs – to Vienna and the other big cities nearby. The regular population was, of course, very unhappy about this; we, on the other hand, not only knew that it was close to lunchtime but were also happy to see the instruments of our liberation.

During lunch one day, we were startled to see a local Austrian woman ride by on her bicycle, looking around very nervously; then, with a sudden movement, she threw a little parcel that landed among us. When we opened it, we saw that it was a prepared barbecued chicken! She must have been keeping watch because she risked being severely punished by the Nazi authorities. We never found out who she was but with that one action she had shown her humanity, letting us know that she didn't support the Nazis or the idea that just because we were born Jewish, we had to be slaves. There were a few more heartwarming occasions like this, which showed us there was decency among the Austrian population.

Life on Sundays, when we had time off, was pretty normal; sometimes I worked on sorting and rearranging my stamp collection. Also, close to our farmhouse was the estate's large mansion, next to which stood a huge barn where exotic circus animals were kept, to safeguard them from the bombing raids in Vienna. On our time off, we were allowed to visit the elephants, tigers, lions, monkeys and zebras.

In the mansion, to my delight, a high society lady stayed with her pretty sixteen-year-old daughter. We grew acquainted, went on dates to see the circus animals and sneaked into the nearby cornfield to enjoy each other's company. Sometimes, on those occasions, I forgot the dire situation I was living in, and I felt like a carefree teenager. I'm sure that if her high society mother found out about our dating adventures, all hell would have broken loose. My mother, however, noticed it and just smiled to herself that her son had some pleasant relief from the slave labour situation.

As time passed, we harvested and gathered the crops; it was hard work. The Leib boy and I had grown stronger and were ordered to work in the wheat harvesting process. We rode on a tractor, driven by one of the Soviet POWs, that pulled a harvesting machine that cut and baled the wheat. We sat on the edge of the tractor as it moved in a straight line until it reached the end of the field and had to loop around ninety degrees in the other direction. At that point, we had to jump off and run to pick up the bales, moving them safely out of the way so the wheat wouldn't be wasted, then jump back on the tractor and ride to the other corner of the field and repeat the process over and over again.

This work lasted several weeks and as we got to know the strong, grown-up men who were doing the really tough work, we asked them to help get us transferred to work with the threshing machine. We worked with straw first, which was not difficult but it stuck to our bodies in the warm weather and was itchy. Later on we volunteered to help carry wheat from the threshing machine to the warehouse, toting 100-kilogram bags up one, two and sometimes three flights of stairs. It was extremely challenging, but we could rest while we rode on the wagon into the town and back, so it was much easier than hoeing or doing the harvesting by hand in the fields.

This process of harvesting wheat was new to me because in Hungary I had seen the peasants using scythes, cutting swaths about two metres wide with very practised strokes, followed by a person, usually a woman, who gathered it into bales. On the farm, we also used machinery to harvest potatoes – the tractor towed a machine that pulled the potatoes out of the ground and we had to pick them out from the earth and put them into boxes.

We worked on the farm from June through to November 1944. After the wheat and potato harvest, we harvested sugar beets, which was the last crop of the season and went to the very end of November. The weather had started to worsen and working in the rain and mud made our days much more unpleasant, but we were still relatively well off. After we finished the sugar beets – I think the date was November 29 – we were told to gather our belongings and the same foreman took us back to Strasshof, back to the place where he had picked us up in June.

We didn't know what was going to happen to us next. Where would we be sent? We were scared because we had heard from locals, who rarely talked to us, and from the Soviet POWs, that deadly atrocities were being committed against Jews. Nonetheless, we still didn't know about the concentration camps and what was going on there. We had discarded the rumours we heard in Hungary as unbelievable. Surely human beings weren't capable of that type of violence; what we heard had to be just rumours.

We didn't spend long at the Strasshof camp. We were put into cattle cars again and this time we were on the train for about five days or so with only water and a bit of bread, so my mother's foresight now came in handy. Those dried fruits she had prepared helped our entire group stay alive. All four families were given an equal portion to supplement our food, which everybody used extremely sparingly.

On December 7, 1944, we arrived at a large railyard, where we were ordered to get off the train and line up in the usual manner of five to a row. Then we were directed to march, and approximately five kilometres later, we arrived at a large complex surrounded by a barbed-wire fence, watchtowers and SS guards with dogs and machine guns. We had arrived at a concentration camp called Bergen-Belsen.

The Sonderlager

The Bergen-Belsen camp was about halfway between Hannover and Hamburg in northwestern Germany. When we arrived at the gates of the camp in mid-afternoon, the winter weather was bitterly cold, rainy and snowy. I saw a long main street lined with pleasant bunga-low-like buildings on one side – which turned out to be the guards' quarters – then a kitchen complex, and farther down, a dark building with a tall chimney from which black smoke billowed. On the other side of the street were large blocks of barracks separated by barbed wire and in them I later saw hundreds and hundreds of emaciated, staggering and skeletal male and female inmates wearing striped uni-forms made of thin fabric.

The guards led us into the right side of a building where we had to disrobe and shower. Then our clothing and belongings were given back to us and our group was taken to block 11, barracks F. Blocks were known by number, and the barracks within them, by letter. We soon found out that block 11 was a *Sonderlager*, which means special camp. We didn't yet know exactly what that meant and why it was "special," but we soon learned that the very fact that we remained together was unusual; in the other blocks, men and women weren't kept together. It was also different that we were given back our own clothing –everybody else in Bergen-Belsen was dressed in the striped *Häftling* (prisoner) uniform, with no overcoats or other warm clothing. Back at the farm in Hollabrunn, my mother had told me to put my stamps, which I had brought from my album, into small envelopes, and she sewed them into the lining of my jacket. Those stamps survived with me inside my ragged jacket.

After liberation, we found out that our unusual situation was largely due to a single individual, Rezső (Rudolf) Kasztner, a Hungarian Jew originally from Kolozsvár (Cluj), Transylvania. Through his efforts, an unprecedented agreement was reached between some western Jewish organizations and high-ranking SS officers Adolf Eichmann and Kurt Becher. Using bribery, manipulation and cajolery, approximately 30,000 Hungarian Jews would be, as they referred to it, "put on ice" – taken to Austria for slave labour and later exchanged, for money and other goods, to eventually end up in neutral Switzerland. The only condition requested – and agreed to – was that these deportees be remnants of families with children whose fathers were in the forced labour service. Kasztner, as a Hungarian Jew, was negotiating specifically on behalf of Hungarians and since the majority of Europe's Jewry had already been slaughtered, only the Hungarian deportees fit the requirements. In the end, about 18,000 Hungarian Jews were actually brought to Austria.

A very interesting coincidence happened as my mother, grandmother, brothers and I entered the barracks: on a worn-out cabinet, among other words scratched into the wooden surface, I noticed a message that read, "Today Dec.4.1944 they are taking me and my family away from here, we do not know where to. Avrom Jungreis rabbi of Szeged." This had special meaning to us because he was the eldest son of our beloved rabbi from our hometown who had blessed me in Strasshof. He was the same age as my father and had grown up with him, so we knew him and his family very well. My mother and grandmother and I often talked about it later, that we had been so close to seeing him in Bergen-Belsen.

Rabbi Avrom Jungreis and his family were among the nearly 1,700 people from that block who were exchanged on December 4, 1944.

They were part of a different group whose release had been negotiated by Kasztner and, having arrived in Bergen-Belsen on a train from Budapest in July, they had been waiting for the technicalities to be worked out so that they could reach Switzerland. The plan was that the next train – ours – would bring in a similar number of people to be put into the same block for a future exchange. The fact that we were among the Hungarian deportees who had been collected from various slave labour locations in Austria was another miracle for my immediate family and certainly resulted in our survival. As it turned out, though, the exchange of our group never took place, in part because of the advancement of the Allied forces and in part, I think, because of a breakdown in negotiations.

The barracks, which housed around 130 of us, was about ten by fifteen metres, with narrow, triple-decked bunk beds pushed next to each other. The beds were seventy-five centimetres wide and were shared by two people. My mother, two brothers and I slept on the top, on the third level. My grandmother, being older and in poor health, got a single bed close to the entrance, where there were other single beds for people like her who couldn't climb up to the higher beds. There was no heat and the building, made of simple wooden walls, wasn't insulated; if we left a cup of water at the end of our bunk bed at night, in the morning we would find a block of ice.

In our *Sonderlager*, the biggest difference I noticed from other blocks was that we were not forced to work. Every single day, regardless of rain, snow or cold, we were ordered to stand for an *Appell*, a roll call, from about 10:00 a.m. to 2:00 p.m., lined up in columns of five to be counted.

Across the main street from our block was the kitchen complex for the entire concentration camp. SS guards on motorcycles or in cars patrolled the street and prisoners pushed and pulled wagons along it, either with supplies for the kitchen or dead bodies piled on like stacked wood. We soon learned that to our left stood the crematorium, which constantly, day and night, belched out black, horrible-smelling smoke. It was the smell of burning flesh, from Jews and oth-ers – political prisoners or Gypsies (Roma) or other "non-desirable" human beings. Sometimes, looking through the barbed wire, we saw some of the emaciated men who were pulling or pushing the wagons collapse. When that happened, the man was stripped of his clothing, thrown on top of the wagon and taken to the crematorium whether or not he was dead.

Bergen-Belsen didn't have gas chambers, but we later heard that it was infamous for being one of the cruellest of all the concentra-tion camps. Its inmates were annihilated in unprecedented numbers through starvation, illness, sadistic beatings, and by being worked to death. Inmates arrived continually but the population of the camp pretty much stayed the same because of all the deaths. When the cre-matorium couldn't consume all the dead bodies, they were piled up in a mountain near it.

Although those of us living in the *Sonderlager* were given more food than the other camp inmates, this still meant that in the morn-ing we only received about half a litre of brown liquid – called coffee – that was at least lukewarm and helped a bit in the freezing cold. At noon we got some sort of soup that had some potato or beet skins floating in it, and in the evening, again, some coffee-coloured water. For every ten people, we were also given one loaf of bread that was ten by ten by twenty-five centimetres. We could tell that the bread was made from a combination of sawdust, wheat flour and cornmeal, but that was our main staple of the day. It became extraordinarily important to divide it in even slices because starvation was taking its toll even within our *Sonderlager*. We couldn't risk people wanting to kill each other because, in their desperation, they might think that someone else had gotten a bigger piece. So somebody fashioned a kind of a blade to cut the bread into equal pieces so that everybody would have a 100 × 100 × 25 millimetre slice.

Because I had been a cabinetmaker's apprentice before we were deported and as such had learned to measure, cut and judge dimensions properly, I volunteered to cut the bread. That made me an important person in the barracks and the few morsels (they had to be very few) that remained on the table after the slicing were my reward. I knew that if I didn't do a proper job and someone felt that their piece was smaller, I could be lynched. Thankfully, everybody seemed satisfied and having this important job contributed to my survival.

In our block, life – if I could call it that while being imprisoned, stripped of my individuality and dignity – went on but the starvation diet made us all weaker by the day. We only endured because we had been given enough food during our slave labour on the farm and the strength and resilience that we had built up helped slow the devastating effects of hunger. The few pieces of dried fruit that my mother doled out to the five of us helped a little too. With very sparing daily consumption, those dried fruits that we had brought with us lasted for a few months and contributed to the fact that, although we were skeletal when we eventually left the camp, we were still able to move.

It soon became evident just how different our *Sonderlager* was when we didn't experience the level of physical abuse we saw on the other side of the barbed wire dividers. The other prisoners were beaten regularly, without reason, just at the guards' whims. We saw them beaten with rifle butts and sticks, and we saw some of them being shot to death just for not being able to do the work they had been ordered to do.

We were also less restricted in our movements after the 10:00 p.m. curfew and were allowed to leave the barracks to go to the latrines. On a December night during Chanukah in 1944, some young men in our block pretended to go to the latrines and instead came in our barracks near the window close to our bunk beds and entertained us by singing Chanukah and other Hebrew songs – "Maʾoz Tzur," "Hatikva" and "Tumbalalaika," with its repetitive refrain, as well as "Techezakna," with its lyrics translated into Hungarian. The latter song speaks about a time when all the *chalutzim* scattered all over the world will be in the land of the Jews and a Jewish flag will fly at the top of Jerusalem. The majority of us, me included, had never heard it before. Living amidst such hopelessness, hearing its uplifting, heartwarming and inspiring words were the most beautiful, unforgettable experience. Even now, when I think about this moment, I get goosebumps.

Close to Christmas, the children from our block were ordered to go to the commandant's barracks, where they were given little pieces of chocolate or little bags of cookies that had come in packages from the International Red Cross. Again, we found out that the treats were only for our block. Children always welcome presents but in that moment it meant so much more – that they could live a little bit longer.

As the days went by, however, we grew more and more depressed by our surroundings. One day, during a roll call in late December, I noticed something crawling on the back of the person standing in front of me. When I asked the person next to me in a whisper, "What is that?" he answered, "Oh, that's lice." We didn't have proper sanitary facilities, which made lice infestations unavoidable and lice brought typhus, a life-threatening disease that quickly became an epidemic. Soon, people either couldn't get up for roll call or fell while standing in it; they were taken away and never seen again. At my mother's urging, we spent a long time each day searching out the eggs and squashing them between our fingernails to decrease our chances of getting infested with lice; thankfully, we all managed to avoid the deadly typhus illness.

During those dreadful months, so much happened that I can only mention a few incidents. When there weren't any minor chores to do after roll call, we were usually allowed to roam around inside the block. Once, when I was standing by a barbed-wire fence, I saw a group of inmates pushing a wagon filled with red beets toward the kitchen complex. I saw a few pieces fall off, either because a wheel rolled over a stone or an inmate "accidently" shook it, and one rolled toward me. I grabbed it, hid it under my coat and took it to my mother.

Fortunately, none of the guards saw me do it. I was so starved that

I hadn't even thought about the times that I'd seen people get shot for that kind of thing; just seeing the beet rolling my way, I had to pick it up. A few bite-size pieces of that raw beet lasted a couple of days and was a critical additional food source for the five of us. Still, we so lacked vitamins that many of us, including me, were developing scurvy with its festering, open wounds. I still have scars on my legs attesting to my experience with the disease.

On the night of my eighteenth birthday, February 20, 1945, I witnessed something extremely disturbing. Sometime after the 10:00 p.m. curfew we heard agonizing screams coming from outside our barracks. I went over to the window and defrosted a small hole with my breath so I could see the next block, which was about one metre away from the window. I saw a large group of inmates herded in there – already looking to be on the verge of collapse – being beaten with rifle butts and sticks with nails and other metal objects protruding from them. The scene that played out in front of me has forever remained in my mind and caused many nightmares. Just a few feet from my face, a man was savagely beaten by an SS guard using a stick with nails and as he fell down, the guard yelled at him to get up. When the man couldn't, he kept beating him until he died right there and then. We found out later that those men had been driven thousands of kilometres on foot from a forced labour camp in the copper mines of Bor, Yugoslavia during those winter months. I tell this horrific story to the students who visit the Toronto Holocaust Centre to illustrate the fact that such hatred-fuelled incidents like this from my past should never become their future.

Yet, another incident with an SS guard was just the opposite; this guard looked like Popeye – he always had a pipe in his mouth and even his features were similar – and he came in every night at 10:00 p.m. to turn off the lights and order us into our bunks. Each time, he would barely step into the barracks before starting to yell, scream and curse at us but while doing this, he would hand out small chocolate bars to the children. Amidst all the inhumanity, there were individuals who still had human feelings and were capable of demonstrating it.

~

At the end of February 1945 we were transferred from block 11 to block 37, barracks C. My grandmother had been losing strength rapidly and wasn't able to move around without assistance, so she was taken to a so-called hospital barracks instead. There wasn't medication or a better diet there, but some volunteer doctors and nurses tried to ease the suffering of those who were unable to take care of themselves. Everyone there perished fairly quickly, as did my grandmother. I could barely hear her as I bent my ear down, close to her mouth. I later found out that she died two days after we left the camp. Under our circumstances, we couldn't observe the traditional mourning period. Anyone who lost a member of their family was of course pained and saddened, but we all focused on trying to survive one more day and wake up alive the next.

Block 37 was at the very end of the main street, just across from the crematorium. I was now living closest to the place that was constantly fed dead bodies, carted there by the still "living" – or at least functioning – inmates. I don't know why we were transferred to that block; in retrospect, number 37 was a smaller block and perhaps our dwindled numbers didn't warrant us staying in block 11, which had the capacity to hold about 5,000 inmates. At that point, I think 2,000 of our group had died. In addition to being across from the crematorium, we were now housed near an empty field where bodies were piled on top of each other when the crematorium couldn't work fast enough. When we left Bergen-Belsen, that pile was higher than our barracks.

In our new barracks I was asked to continue my job of slicing our daily bread ration. One day, an SS guard came into the barracks around mid-morning and barked an order for a young man to come with him to clean the latrines; he then pointed at me. The unelected leader of the barracks said to him, "Sir, that man has an important job here. He's the one who slices the bread every day. Would it be possible to take someone else?" Instead of hitting this man who dared speak to him, the guard just shrugged and pointed to someone else.

The latrine job involved disrobing and jumping into the refuse pit with a pail that had to be filled and then handed up to other inmates, who put the contents into wagons to be hauled away. Inmates who were too weak to do the job often collapsed and drowned, right there in the refuse. The body was just thrown up into the wagon. That young man taken instead of me never returned. Was he shot because he wasn't able to do it or was he one of those who collapsed and drowned? We never found out. I could have been that person, perishing there and then. As I mentioned before, unforeseeable and unexplainable miracles were the only reason that I managed to survive that hell on earth.

We grew weaker day by day. Not only were our bodies deteriorating, but our clothing was as well – my pants were torn to shreds. My mother made a pair of pants for me from potato sacks that we somehow got from the kitchen barracks; my jacket, as thin as it was, was still in one piece with the stamps in the little envelopes inside. Those of us who were still alive could at least hope for our liberation – rumours were starting to go around that the end of the war was near. The Allied bombers' flights above us were more frequent and many a time we heard rumblings, which were either exploding bombs or artillery noises indicating that the front was moving closer.

On the morning of April 7, 1945, we were told to get our belongings and line up in front of our barracks. We soon realized that we were being herded out on the same road by which we came into the camp. I found out later that because of the progression of the war, the Germans were planning to take us all to the Theresienstadt concentration camp, a place still under Nazi control. At this point they were still hoping to negotiate our exchange with the Allies.

Only four months earlier, we had been strong enough to march into the camp, but now we were starving and skeletal, and could only shuffle out. As fate or the will of God arranged, since we were in barracks C and the column to empty the block proceeded alphabetically, we were near the front. As the march progressed, however, we were so feeble that we started to fall behind and meld into other groups. Since my mother and I were the weakest among the four of us, some of our barracks mates, noting that we seemed to be heading to the same railyard where we came in, offered to take my two younger brothers with them and secure a spot for us. While hugging them goodbye, just in case we got separated, we heard shots and when we looked back, we saw that people who couldn't keep up had been shot on the spot. Even so, for the next few hours, my mother and I often had to pause and rest before we could continue. We started out at seven o'clock and somewhere around one or two in the afternoon, we started to see the group thinning because the last group had already gone by. Somehow, though, we managed to reach the railyard as part of the very last group. Had we started out in the middle or the back of the column, we surely would have been shot. The people who accompanied my brothers were pleasantly surprised to see us – they hadn't thought that they would see us again.

Before I climbed up to the wagon where my relieved brothers were waiting, I saw that a few train tracks away there was an open railcar loaded with red beets and that people from our group were stealing a few of them. I asked my mother to dump everything out of one of our pillowcases, dragged myself to the railcar and took as many beets as I could carry – maybe half a dozen or so – and started back to our wagon. When I got to the track next to ours, I saw an SS guard with his back to me lift his machine gun and shoot a small boy, maybe ten or eleven years old, who was holding a red beet in each hand. In the eyes of that SS guard, stealing two beets deserved the death penalty. I quickly handed my loot to someone who passed it to my mother, so when that SS guard turned around, I was just standing there. He just barked at me to climb back into the wagon, which I did. Had he turned around ten or fifteen seconds earlier, my fate would have been the same as that little boy's.

After the cattle wagons' doors were closed, with the usual amount of crowding, the train started to move. We were on that train to the unknown for six days. We were given hardly any food, so those red beets basically sustained us. While the train was proceeding, mainly during the nights but even sometimes during the days, we heard Allied planes flying overhead.

In addition to our cattle wagons, the train's twenty cars included a regular coach for the officers and the SS guards and three open cars with anti-aircraft guns mounted on them – one near the front, one in the middle and one at the end. The guns fired on the Allied planes, but fortunately no bombs fell on our train. At the time, we thought it was a miracle, but after liberation, I heard, but was never able to confirm, that the Allies knew who was in that train because they had been photographing our procession since we left Bergen-Belsen.

On the fifth day of our journey, April 12, a Thursday afternoon, we were about fifteen kilometres from Magdeburg, a city on the Elbe River about halfway between Berlin and Hannover. The train stopped on a curve near a bridge over the river, which wasn't unusual, since a red light frequently stopped the train for a short period. This time, however, there wasn't any movement. We later found out that the Nazis had devised a new plan – they wanted to position the train on the bridge and blow it up so that they could both kill us and stop the Allied advance. Somehow, though, the engineer and his assistant had gotten wind of the plan. They, too, must have heard the rumbling explosions from the front line and realized that the end of the war was imminent. Not wanting to die, they just ran off while the train was stopped at the red light, leaving the train and its cargo behind.

After a while the guards opened all the doors and the commandant ordered all males above the age of twelve to get out of the wagons and go over to a little embankment across from the train. Then, while we were facing our respective cattle wagons that contained our family members, a machine gun was set up in front of each wagon. Not every machine gun was manned by an SS guard. We stood there facing the machine guns – and death – for a couple of hours; then, inexplicably, the guns were removed and we were ordered to return to our wagons.

Even now, I do not know for sure what happened, but I think, just through hearsay, that so close to the end of the war, the guards couldn't be forced to carry out executions – they had to volunteer. Very fortunately for us, only eight SS guards volunteered and I guess the commandant wouldn't dare try to carry out his plan with so few men. It is a very sad fact that all those volunteers were vehement anti-semites from Hungary, our own native land.

That night, a fierce air battle developed around and above our train. The guns were blazing, bombs were falling and explosions were shaking our wagons, but again, none of them fell on us. In the morning, the first thing we noticed was there were no SS guards – they had fled during the night, leaving us to our fate, which turned out to be our salvation. These are things that I cannot explain, that no one can explain, but to me it looks like God was looking after us and creating these miracles.

People were milling around outside of the wagons, talking about what had happened. Sometime around midday, I had made a fire from some twigs and I was starting to boil some of the remaining red beets in a pot when suddenly a huge cry went up. When I looked over to the top of that little embankment, I saw some dirty, sweating American soldiers – the most beautiful human beings imaginable – appear with their guns ready. Instead of the enemy, they found us and heard our screams and our cries of "Oh God, we are free! We are going to be human beings again!"

We were liberated near the village of Farsleben, about twenty kilometres north of Magdeburg, on Friday, April 13, 1945, at around 1:00 p.m. (and therefore, ever since then, I call Friday the thirteenth my very, very lucky day). I remember going back and forth between that pot of beets and the door of the wagon, telling my mother and brothers that we were free, crying at the same time. That feeling was not, and still is not, possible to express in words. After more than sixty years, whenever I think about that moment, my skin still shivers. Those soldiers from the Ninth United Sates Army not only liberated us, they gave us back our lives.

Liberation

The first thing that the American soldiers said to us was that we were truly free and that whoever was able should come with them. Me and my eleven-year-old brother, George, were helped up onto the little embankment where we could see a road leading to a small town about three hundred metres away. The Americans had already ordered all the townspeople to leave their houses, so they were either in their backyards, barns or other outbuildings.

Inside the houses, the soldiers indicated that we should take whatever we wanted. One soldier led me to a wardrobe and showed me lots of beautiful suits, gesturing for me to choose what I liked. There was a delicious smell of food coming from the kitchen, where I saw dishes filled with food – normal, human food! The people who lived there must have been having their lunch when they were forcibly evacuated. George and I immediately started stuffing ourselves and then packed some of the food into pots. I also found a two or three-litre pot filled with prune butter and brought that to my mother and Frank. They started eating it right away, but my mother, extraordinarily smart and practical as always, controlled herself and told my younger brother to eat only a small amount. She wouldn't let me or George eat any more either, since we told her we had eaten earlier.

That night, many of us who had gorged ourselves on the food we found, including me and George, became violently ill. Our mother forced her finger down into our throats, relieving our stomachs and saving our lives. Unfortunately, about two hundred people of the roughly 2,500 from our train didn't have my mother's foresight and died because their bodies couldn't digest the amount of regular food that they ate in the days immediately following our liberation. We didn't know the medical term for this, so we called it starvation or hunger typhus because its victims died as quickly and in the same numbers as they had in the concentration camp. A cemetery was created in the nearby town of Hillersleben for those unfortunate victims, whose demise was even more painful because they had just regained their freedom; they had survived, so briefly, the Nazi regime.

The next day the soldiers drove us to Hillersleben, an upscale community that had housed the families of high-ranking German officers. They were also ordered to vacate their homes – just as we were when we had been forced into the ghettos – and their homes became our quarters for the next several months as the American medical corps slowly brought our digestive systems back to normal.

The American army then began the tedious task of properly identifying us. They painstakingly recorded everybody's personal data to establish what country each person was from and what family members had survived with them. I still have the certificate that the Ninth Army issued to me with my photograph from a few years earlier attached to it.

By coincidence, the army chaplain rabbi who belonged to this division of the Ninth Army was a man from New York named Meisels. When this chaplain saw our name on the list of the liberated survivors, he came to our quarters to talk to us. Although I didn't speak a word of English, I spoke German fairly fluently and we were able to converse. Rabbi Meisels' hobby was genealogy and he was very interested to find out what we knew about our family's origins. From my father's stories, my mother and I could tell him that seven generations earlier, in the second half of the eighteenth century in Munkacs in northeastern Hungary – which between the two world wars was part of Czechoslovakia and is now part of the Ukraine – there was a very poor Meisels family with more mouths to be fed than food was available. Among those numerous children were six or seven sons, who decided, as many from that region in those days did, that their future would look brighter if they went to America.

Hearing this piqued his interest, so we continued, telling him that poor people used to walk from one town to the next offering to do work for a day or so in return for food and shelter. For Orthodox Jews, if they ended up in a Jewish community on a Friday evening, they went to the synagogue. At the end of the service, as was the custom, families invited them to their homes for Shabbat. On Sunday, after the morning prayers, they would start their journey to the next town.

When the Meisels brothers reached Nádudvar in north-central Hungary, they were on their way to Trieste, Italy, which was the nearest ocean port. From there, travellers often offered to work on the ships for their fare across the ocean. On one particular Sunday morning, however, one of the brothers told the others that there was a beautiful girl at the home where he had stayed for Shabbat, and that he had fallen in love with her. With her parents' blessing, he hoped to marry her. He had found his "America" and was staying. That man was my great-great grandfather's great-grandfather. The other brothers continued their journey and ended up in America as they had planned. When the rabbi heard this, he grew very excited and said that his research tallied with my story and that he was the descendant of one of those brothers as well. Unfortunately we lost contact, even though I tried to find him again.

When the war officially ended in May and Germany was to be divided into four Allied zones, the territory of Hillersleben was to become part of the Soviet zone. Rabbi Meisels asked us to go back to New York with him and said that he would help us gain entry to the United States. That kind of offer was a dream for many survivors but, for us, it was unrealistic; we had to decline because we didn't know my father's fate. Was he still alive? We had to go back to Hungary to find out.

That decision, like the one I made when I forced my family to come with me on the train that ended up in Austria instead of Auschwitz, altered our future. Looking back, our decision was not the most rational one because if my father had survived he would have been able to follow us to America; if he had perished, what reason would there be to go back to our home country? We had lived our lives there as patriotic citizens only to have a large segment of the population turn against us and cooperate with the Nazis to murder us. As fate determined, we did eventually end up in North America but how different our lives would have been if we had gone earlier, no one can ever know.

In August, the Soviets organized our transportation back to Hungary but the return journey was neither straightforward nor smooth. Although they put us in regular train coaches, somewhere west of Dresden, which I admit I was happy to see destroyed, for some reason we had to disembark in a little town. We were given temporary accommodations in the attics of homes or barns until another train arrived to continue the journey to Hungary.

In the attic where we stayed, there was a small group of young women survivors who had been liberated from the Ravensbrück concentration camp. They were also on their way to their homes in Hungary and one of them, Magda Friedman, was a first cousin of my father. Someone from our extended family had survived! From there on, we continued the journey together. Magda was an unmarried young woman who, like us, was anxious to reach her home and find out if any of her family survived. She only knew that her parents had been taken to the Budapest ghetto and her brother to a forced labour camp.

On the morning of September 10, 1945 – my brother George's twelfth birthday – our train stopped at a railyard on the outskirts of Budapest and my cousin and I went to use the telephone in the office. When Magda tried her parents' number, amazingly, they answered! Her parents had survived the Holocaust in the Budapest ghetto and had been liberated in January. But the wonderful, miraculous news didn't end there. When she told them that she had met up with us and that we were together, they told her that my father was also among the few who survived and that he was in Nádudvar! They said that they would send a telegram immediately to let him know that we had come back.

We hadn't known about my father's survival until the day we arrived in Budapest, but he had heard through the international Red Cross and Jewish organizations in May that we had survived, so he was eagerly awaiting word from us. On the day our telegram arrived, he was out working the fields and when he saw his brother-in-law, Sandor Grosz, coming toward him on his bicycle, he yelled to him, "They are home, aren't they?" He immediately got on the bicycle, left his horses for Sandor and got on the next train to meet us at his aunt's home in Budapest.

Our reunion was joyous. There are no words to describe the feeling that from the ashes and the shadows of the crematorium, from a living hell, we were now all together, alive. Miracles, fate or the will of God, or maybe the combination of all three, had helped us survive. I was one of the very few whose entire immediate family survived the Holocaust. However, like everyone, we had lost numerous relatives – my grandmother, aunts, uncles, cousins – who had perished in the gas chambers or in the forced labour camps.

The story of my father's survival was unusual. Out of all of those men with whom he was called up when Mr. Papp was able to release him, barely any returned at the end of the war. My father had had the good fortune to be put in a group of about 250 men whose commanding lieutenant was a teacher in Egyek, a town fifty kilometres from Nádudvar, and his soldiers, who were actually their guards, were reservists drafted from the same area. This commanding officer wasn't antisemitic and sympathized with the men under his command. His attitude influenced his troops, who also behaved decently toward their charges.

The lieutenant decided to form a committee from all the men who had previously been officers, as well as a few elders, to carry out whatever orders they needed to follow. He figured this would make everything go more smoothly. My father, although not an officer in his regular army service, was forty-four years old and therefore an elder, so he became part of that group.

Their committee's first jobs involved repairing the bombed-out airport runways and roads in and around Debrecen. Sometime in August, as the advancing Soviet army neared the Hungarian border, they received an order to abandon their quarters and start marching toward Germany. My father, experienced, logical and smart, had an idea that he discussed with the committee members, who welcomed it; since he had also developed a good rapport with the commander, my father approached him as well. "Sir," he said, "I know that you were born in a town near mine and lived your life up to now on the east side of the Tisza River like I did, and all of us in your group are from around this area. Would it not be better that if we have to die, we die on this side rather than west of the river or in Germany?"

The commander responded that although he could understood how the men felt, how could they disobey the order in his hand? My father then suggested a way around it: they could appear to be following orders by marching along the Tisza River toward Tiszafüred, where there was a bridge to cross to the west side, but before they reached the bridge, they would turn back and start marching toward Tokaj and Fegyvernek, where there were other bridges. Since the retreating German, as well as some Hungarian, army units were constantly moving toward these bridges, the commander would answer any questions by saying that he had to get these Jews to Germany but had been turned back at the crossing to give troops the priority, and had to go to another bridge.

The commander accepted my father's proposal, knowing that the army retreat was urgent and that the likelihood of meeting the same interrogators twice was remote. They stopped at various large farms for days, sometimes for weeks, where plenty of food was available because the crops and livestock couldn't be shipped to the cities and markets. They would then continue marching, always staying within an eighty-kilometre range of Nádudvar. They roamed the countryside until the first of November, when the area was liberated by the Soviet army.

The commandant's cooperation with my father and the other Jews allowed him and his troops to live through those hard times. His group was one of the few that weren't sent to the Soviet front, driven by their guards toward the minefields and blown up to clear the way for the German and Hungarian troops, or taken to Germany and put into concentration camps. Their wanderings had been dangerous and nerve-racking and four men reached the point where they couldn't bear it any longer and escaped to Budapest, hoping to reach the ghetto where they thought they would be safe. Unfortunately, they were caught either by the Nazis or the Arrow Cross and were the only casualties of that forced labour group.

My hometown was liberated by the Soviet army on November 3, 1944, and my father and a friend from his group hitchhiked their way there, arriving home as free men on the following day, November 4. The fascist-leaning antisemitic leaders had fled and were replaced by left-leaning socialists and some previously imprisoned communists, among whom were quite a few of my father's friends from the regular army units. When they heard that he was home, they immediately sent for him and, knowing his capabilities, asked him to organize a convoy, transport wheat to Nagyvárad, which was about seventy kilometres away, and barter it for salt, iron bars for wagon wheels, and petroleum. Normal commerce did not yet exist, and there was a dire need for these items. They hadn't been available for quite a while and many people were so desperate for them that they walked five kilometres to a well that contained a salty mineral. Nagyvárad, which had reverted back to Romanian control after the war, was located in a salt-producing area that also had plenty of oil wells and Romania was in need of wheat. My hometown area, in a fertile, wheat-growing region, had hundreds of loads of wheat that hadn't been shipped out because of the war. All the warehouses, most of the abandoned Jewish homes, and the schools were filled to the ceiling with wheat.

At the Soviets' request, the municipal leaders lined up townspeople every day for work in whatever area the military needed. They suggested that my father choose ten or fifteen people with horses and wagons to be exempt from those daily tasks and load their wagons with wheat. At that time, however, the Soviet troops were still advancing toward the frontlines and were seizing horses, sometimes along with their drivers and loads. Knowing this, my father agreed to take on the job on one condition: that the town leaders provide a couple of armed Soviet soldiers to accompany them as protection. This request was met.

The first convoy was so successful that my father was asked to continue, which he did until normal commerce was re-established months later. During this time, my father suggested that the municipal leaders exempt several blacksmiths and carriage-makers from the daily workforce and order them back to their shops to make a large transport vehicle using locally available wood components and wheels; other necessities, like rubber wheels, ball bearings and suspensions could be salvaged from the shot-up German, Hungarian and Soviet tanks that littered the countryside. With two strong horses, that wagon was capable of carrying five times the weight of a regular wagon. This considerably increased the capacity of the convoys.

After the convoys fulfilled their purpose and normal commerce resumed, my father purchased that trailer from the municipality and a pair of strong horses to establish a transport company that mainly hauled goods for the local merchants from Debrecen. He also leased some acreage of land where he grew wheat, corn and hay for his horses. By the time we got home, his new business was prospering.

Before the war, we had rented a house for many years, but after we were deported it was rented to someone else. So when my father arrived home, he went to his parents' house, which he found completely empty, just the four walls in each room. Strangely, all our furniture appeared the next morning at the synagogue's front entrance. He never found out who had taken it and who had returned it, but it meant a lot to my father because his uncle had made that furniture for my parents when they got married.

During his first days at home, my father heard that Molnar, the murderous butcher's apprentice who was a member of the Arrow Cross Party, was living at home with his parents as a free man; he had never been punished for his crimes. The Soviet army was arresting Nazi collaborators and sending them to work in the Siberian coal mines for years; my father now had enough clout that Molnar was in the next group sent to those mines. He didn't die there, as many did, but about five years later he returned home looking much older and broken in body and soul. He had finally gotten his due punishment.

What Would Our Future Hold?

After we returned from the concentration camp, my life felt rather complicated. I was a young man who had matured to some degree but my development had been anything but normal. The psychological effects of my experiences taught me certain things that formed a philosophy that I have lived by ever since. Life in the concentration camp, especially watching the leadership in our barracks and acquiring the simple knowledge of how to measure and cut bread rations precisely, taught me a great deal. I saw how people who were well educated and broad-minded stood out from the crowd, how they were able to adapt to their situation more easily than others. People looked up to them and they became leaders. I came to the conclusion that no matter what circumstance life puts a person in, even if everything you have is taken away, as long as you live, no one can take away your knowledge. Everything you have learned remains yours and can help you. For me, this produced a thirst for knowledge and a will to learn, which has never changed.

As a result, in the fall of 1945, immediately after I returned home, I re-started my cabinetmaker apprenticeship and enrolled in night school to continue my education. I worked on enhancing my education until I left Hungary.

I had three months left in my apprenticeship before I could take my trade exams and receive my certificate as a cabinetmaker journeyman, and I was fortunate to be able to finish my apprenticeship with Morris Straussman, my old master. He had been on the same transport to Austria and survived a period of slave labour near Vienna; he was liberated in the Theresienstadt camp. He had returned earlier than us and was able to restart his business. At the end of December 1945, I successfully passed my exam and, after receiving my designation, continued to work for him as a well-paid journeyman.

I am convinced that I became a better-educated and broader-minded person after the war. If I had continued to live my life just the same way as I had before the war, I wouldn't have had the same kind of insights about life, often in crucial moments. After the Holocaust, I started my new life by seeing, judging and appreciating people the way they are and the way they behave, live and conduct themselves.

~

Life after the war wasn't as smooth as many people would have liked. By the spring of 1946 Hungary still hadn't recovered economically and inflation rose dramatically, somewhat similar to the way it had in 1923, after World War I. The difference was that this inflation was higher, with millions, billions and trillions of denominations; the prices increased to denominations of money that no one could even pronounce. It was called adó (tax) pengő, after the name of the Hungarian currency. Around May, inflation reached a level where my wages became worth almost nothing – for a week's work I could only buy a loaf of bread. Since my father's business was progressing, we decided it would be better for me to join him instead of continuing my work as a journeyman cabinetmaker.

In July 1946, just a week or two before the revaluation of the currency (to slow down and stop the inflation), I wanted to take the train to see my uncle Josef Grossman, who lived about eighty kilometres from us. My mother gave me two eggs to take to the market and I jumped on my bicycle, sold them for whatever the going rate was (hundreds of trillions of pengős), then went on to the railroad station to buy a return ticket for the next day. The railroad raised its ticket prices every day because the government set new prices at midnight, but by midday, with the values changing by the hour, I had money left over after getting my tickets to buy some magazines too. Normally, not even ten dozen eggs would buy a one-way ticket.

The inflation affected many peoples' earnings and destroyed their savings, but living in a relatively small agricultural town provided a buffer against complete economic ruin – people bartered whatever they grew and exchanged those items for other goods. My father's sharp mind helped us through this time; he charged a certain amount of salt for shipments, rather than money. This salt, which never lost its value, could be exchanged for goods, and traded in for money at a later date. Fortunately for the country and its people, the government successfully stopped the inflation and re-established a relatively solid currency on August 1, 1946.

Almost immediately after I joined my father in the transportation business, we acquired more merchants as customers, including some from the three neighbouring towns of Kaba, Földes and Tetétlen, which were possible to service on the way home from Debrecen. We added more horses and another trailer, and our business grew.

One Sunday afternoon, a storeowner's wife came to our house to say that her husband had come down with the flu and wouldn't be able to go to Debrecen by train to do his buying rounds. They were hoping that if they paid my train fare, I would be willing to travel ahead of the carriage and do the buying for them. She brought the list of what they needed and a bundle of money and I naturally complied. When other people heard about this, they came to us and said they would prefer to use their time in their stores rather than spending it on buying, so we started to offer that as an additional, no-charge service. Many of our customers used it and reduced their trips to the distributors to once a month rather than having to go weekly. We further benefitted because I could buy similar items at one place instead of different locations with competitive pricing. That reduced our loading time and work, and some distributors offered a small percentage of commission to me as well, which didn't affect the price the customers had to pay for their goods.

Our attitude toward rebuilding our lives was that whenever anybody called us, day or night, any hour, six days a week, we were ready to go. After liberation, we weren't as religiously observant as before, but we still didn't work on Saturdays, nor did our helpers. On Friday nights, we tried to be home by candle lighting.

Both of my brothers had their bar mitzvahs after the war. With an additional six men in town, we were able to form a minyan, a religious quorum, so on Saturday mornings and High Holidays we kept services in a small, restored portion of the synagogue. We didn't use the larger part of the synagogue because the Germans had used it as a warehouse and stable and had left only the bare walls.

Our congregation had been strictly Orthodox before the deportation, forced labour and concentration camps; after the war, many were not. Survivors were questioning the existence of God and some turned away from religion. My family had experienced so many miracles that we remained firm believers in the supreme power, even with our less religious practices.

By the end of 1949, many of the surviving families had either moved away from Nádudvar to Debrecen or Budapest, or immigrated to Israel and other countries. The religious services were no longer given. A couple years later, my father suggested that the town sell the synagogue to the municipality and donate the proceeds to the fairly large Jewish community of Debrecen; in return, they would maintain the Jewish cemetery when there weren't any Jews left in Nádudvar. The Jewish leaders in Debrecen accepted and although it wasn't customary to sell synagogues for non-religious purposes, my father offered the building and land to the town, which would demolish it and use the bricks to build a fence around the sports stadium. At least the synagogue's materials would service the townspeople. After several centuries, this was the end of the Jewish community in Nádudvar.

It was during this same time that the ruling Communist regime, with its atheistic ideology, started to suppress all religious practices. We slowly began to abandon Saturday as a day of rest and adapted to resting on Sundays. However, since we weren't Christians, if somebody wanted our business services on a Sunday, we would agree. We then became a company that operated seven days a week. Our business was so prosperous that in 1948 and 1949 we had two trailers and three pairs of horses so that one could always be resting, as well as some extra helpers. My father took me on as a partner and registered the second trailer in my name. We were contemplating the purchase of a modern tractor to pull the trailers, the kind farmers use in North America nowadays, with rubber wheels and greater speed, to grow our business further. We also considered approaching additional towns and merchants in the surrounding area as prospective customers.

The political climate was changing tremendously. The Cold War was underway and Hungary, having being liberated by the Soviets, became a satellite country. Since 1945, the Communist Party had been implementing a system similar to the one that existed in the Soviet Union, which meant that the state started nationalizing businesses – at first only the larger businesses, but step-by-step, smaller and smaller private enterprises were taken over as well. At the same time, small landowners were forced to join communal agricultural groups.

By 1949, the Communist Party had completely taken over the government. With great difficulty and muted resentments, small storeowners and farmers joined the Soviet-style, state-organized cooperatives. An enterprising middle class hadn't existed in the Soviet Union before the Communist regime, but in Hungary, small business, trade shops and landowners were ambitious, hard-working and very protective of their possessions. Now, people were forced to work other people's land instead of their own because under the Soviet system, everything was "ours" rather than "mine." Taking care of shared implements and other possessions lost the personal touch and machinery and livestock was abused; as a result, productivity decreased instead of the intended increase. These prevailing conditions were the prelude to the 1956 revolution and for us, they meant that we had to revise our plans and couldn't expand our business.

In 1950, these forced cooperatives reached the stage that – even though we had two registered businesses – we were in danger of being taken over by the state. Luckily, my father's good relationship with the leaders of the town helped us out. In the spring of that year, one of the communist leaders came to our house and told my father that a telegram had arrived stating that people from Debrecen would be arriving in a few days to take over our business. We wouldn't receive any compensation. The man told us, "The only successful farming cooperative wants to buy your operation for a fair price and if you sell it to them today, then the others from Debrecen will have come here for nothing." We would be able to manage by selling only two pairs of horses and one trailer, so we sold my registered business and my father's remained below the takeover level. My father and I signed the paperwork and funds were transferred. Luck was with us again and we got through that state ownership plan without economic ruin.

My father continued his business at reduced capacity for two more years, still as a private entrepreneur. At that point, the same people warned my father that the state takeovers had now reached his level and that it would be better to once again sell to the same people. He followed their advice and we put the money from the sale under my mother's pillow. Now, however, my father didn't have a job.

After the sale of my business, close to the wheat harvest, I had started working for the town's largest merchandising cooperative. I was the first person assigned to manage the finance department and was later trained to evaluate the quality of the wheat brought in by the cooperatives and by the few still-existing individual landowners. Eventually, I became supervisor of all the warehouses in town. After several improvement courses, I supervised the warehouses in other districts as well.

My father was only unemployed for a short period and was soon approached by an official from a state-owned company in Debrecen that purchased cattle from small individual owners and the farming cooperatives. The company operated large farms where they improved the quality of beef cattle as much as possible for export, keeping the rest for local butchering. Exporting products and cattle, mainly to West Germany, was crucial to the currency-hungry regime and enterprises that provided goods for export were valued and appreciated by the state.

The man who approached him knew that my father had been a butcher and had the experience they needed, so he offered him management of one of their larger farms some forty kilometres away, which would require my father to commute daily by train. He liked the job offer, but not the commuting part, so he suggested that they set up a farm in Nádudvar. The company official said that his proposal was impractical because they only set up their farms on large estates with the facilities to house hundreds of cattle and there was no such place in our town. In response, my father said, "If you allow me, I will organize a system where the company will be able to fulfill its purpose successfully here in town on relatively small premises with qualified people."

While the small farmers were forced into agricultural cooperatives, those who owned hundreds of acres had their operations taken over and run by the state. Many of their fair-size barns were not being used and that was where my father planned to set up. He knew that it would take some extra effort to operate in more than one place, but he was certain of his ability to be productive, and he knew the right people in town to hire. The state organization needed him, so they agreed to go ahead and let him prove his worth. My father worked hard, getting up every morning at 3:00 or 4:00 a.m. to do the supervising rounds of the necessary feedings; later in the day he rested at home and in the evening he repeated his rounds again. Within a relatively short time, he was the highest producer and exporter of quality beef cattle, first in the province and eventually in the entire country. I was so proud when he was driven to Budapest numerous times to meet with the minister of agriculture and he received many awards from the ministry and from his company, as well as sizable monetary bonuses and premiums.

Both our jobs went relatively smoothly until the fall of 1956, when the revolution against state ownership and dictatorship reached a crescendo. My family had to make an incredibly difficult decision. My middle brother, George, wasn't living at home then. He had graduated from the technical university of Budapest as a mechanical engineer and was working in Debrecen. He had also just gotten married that summer. My younger brother, Frank, was serving his two-year compulsory service in the army. Every healthy young male from twenty years of age was called up to serve in the military and Frank was just finishing when the revolution took place in October 1956.

Before the revolution, the border was sealed and it was nearly impossible to emigrate from any communist country; suddenly it was possible to leave. The border with Austria opened for a short while and tens of thousands of people left their homes, their families and the country. So much did people desire to escape the totalitarian dictatorship that out of an approximate population of nine million, 200,000 – among them at least 10,000 Jews – left Hungary.

At the beginning, crossing over to the west was easy, but after the Soviets crushed the revolution on November 4, 1956, border patrols were reinstated and reinforced with Soviet troops. From then on, escape became dangerous, even life-threatening, though some still bribed people who lived close to the border and managed to get out.

My own decision to leave, along with my brothers, came relatively late. We didn't want to leave at first; we didn't even think about it because we were so rooted in the community. My father was fifty-six and my mother was fifty-two – they didn't want to restart life in a strange place without knowing the language. Their native country had, after the war, provided them with a relatively good livelihood and a lot of respect. After surviving the Holocaust and being among the very few whose whole family had survived, it was extremely difficult for any of us to imagine taking it apart.

Eventually, though, George came home and said that we, too, should leave Hungary and go to the West. We still didn't want to go, but, in addition to the political upheaval, what prompted us to leave was the disturbing news about antisemitic incidents in the bigger cities. Slogans like "This time, Jews, we will not take the trouble to take you to Auschwitz" could be heard or seen painted on walls.

We decided we would leave under one condition – that our parents sell their home and move into my sister-in-law's mother's home in Debrecen. She was older than my parents, close to sixty, and my parents would be able to help support and protect her. Then, after we moved to the West and established ourselves, they would legally be able to follow and bring our families together again.

On December 9, 1956, Frank, George, his new wife, Veronica, and I risked our lives and left from Budapest. We approached the border area by late afternoon, arriving at the rail station in Győr, the largest city between Budapest and the border town of Hegyeshalom. Suddenly, police units boarded the train and looked over the passengers, picking out several hundred of us and ordering us off the train. We were all directed to march toward the city's police station to be registered. We hoped that we wouldn't be charged, but we knew it was likely that we'd be sent back.

As we were walking, a local gentleman came up beside me and asked, "Did you want to go over?" meaning, did I want to escape to Austria. When I answered yes, he told me to step out of line and go with him. We weren't being guarded, so my family followed discreetly and he took us to his house, where, on the inside of the door, we saw a mezuzah. We slept on some blankets on his living room floor and the next day, in the early afternoon, he took us to a smaller, less guarded railway stop and told us the name of a fisherman in a small town near the border who we could bribe to take us to Austria. He didn't give us his name, fearing reprisal in case we were caught and forced to reveal him to the authorities; to this day I'm sorry for that because I never had the opportunity to express our gratitude.

We arrived in the town he had told us to go to in the late afternoon and found the fisherman who, for a considerable sum of money, agreed to smuggle us across Lake Fertő that night, which the countries' border bisected, and get us to Austria, to freedom. Late that evening, as we were waiting for the proper time for our departure, something quite scary happened. The door opened and a young soldier in a border patrol uniform entered. We thought, This is it, the fisherman took our money and gave us up to the authorities. To our delight, however, it turned out that the young man was courting one of the man's daughters and was well aware of his clandestine activities. He had come to tell him what time he and his patrol would be at the lake so we could avoid them.

Around midnight, in total silence, we left the house and followed the man along a small path to his rowboat. After rowing for a considerable time, he announced that there was a small channel amid the cane plants and when we reached land, we would be in Austria. We reached land a few minutes later, where he docked and then left. It was still dark and until dawn we remained in limbo, not knowing if we really were in Austria or if he had just left us somewhere in Hungary. Thankfully, he was an honorable man who had fulfilled his agreement. I'm sure that he also knew that if he had betrayed us, word would have gotten out and that would have been the end of his lucrative side business.

When the sun came up, we saw an Austrian border patrol, which confirmed that we were on Austrian soil. The guards put us on a truck, drove us to Vienna and dropped us off at the Rothschild Hospital, an overcrowded registration station for people fleeing from Hungary.

By this time, it was no longer easy to obtain an entry visa to the US, where we wanted to go to because my uncle Josef lived there. He and his family had managed to immigrate to the US in 1947 and were living in Manchester, Connecticut. Unless we chose another country, we might have to wait a long time for a visa to the US. Many other countries were accepting refugees, but since we wanted to be with our uncle, we decided to wait it out. My sister-in-law, however, was pregnant with their first child and she and George didn't want the child to be born in a refugee camp. She had an aunt living in Brantford, Ontario, so they applied to go to Canada. We looked at a map and figured that since Toronto and Connecticut weren't that far apart, we could reunite after we made it to the US. George and Veronica were accepted right away because of Veronica's pregnancy and were flown to Toronto within a week.

Frank and I remained in Vienna, waiting. We soon found out that the Austrian government, together with the Hebrew Immigrant Aid Society (HIAS) and the American Jewish Joint Distribution Committee, which we called the Joint, were setting up a camp for Jewish refugees in an abandoned World War II military barracks in the city of Korneuburg. The city was about twenty kilometres outside Vienna and there were frequent trains between them, which would make it easy to travel to embassies or the offices of other organizations. We applied, got accepted and moved in.

The conditions in Korneuburg were much better than they had been at the Rothschild Hospital. A kitchen was set up with food supplies and the Red Cross distributed clothing from donations from the US. Still, there were about six hundred refugees there and we were quartered in a large room with bunk beds where thirty-two of us – men, women, couples and families with children – all lived together. Departures were very slow.

We soon learned that tradespeople could get jobs through the local Austrian government employment office and earn money. This would make the wait more bearable. I have to give credit to the Austrian authorities for their employment rules because those of us who could provide our trade certificates got paid the exact same hourly rate as the native Austrians.

My brother, a tool-and-die maker, and I, a cabinetmaker, were among the first half a dozen or so people who got jobs and started work. Frank worked in Vienna and I found employment in a nearby little town called Karnabrunn. From then on we gladly paid the office of the refugee camp thirty shillings per week from our earned wages. With my ten years' experience – not mentioning that I had been out of the trade for a number of years – I earned eight shillings per hour, so I made 320 shillings per week and my brother earned a similar wage. We were both able to put quite a bit into savings.

Coincidentally, I got that job on Wednesday, February 20, 1957 – my thirtieth birthday. That morning I had been lying on my bunk bed looking at the ceiling, feeling almost depressed, asking myself whether I had made the right decision in leaving my life, my job and my parents for this uncertain present and more uncertain future. Then, I got a message to report to the employment office, where I was introduced to a master cabinetmaker from Karnabrunn who needed an additional employee. Naturally, I happily accepted the job. He drove me to his shop and suggested that I stay in his house until Friday. If, at that point, both of us were satisfied, then I would get a monthly train pass the following week to travel to his shop daily. After lunch, I started work in the shop, not knowing if I would meet his expectations. Even when I stood next to the workbench and took the tools in my hand, I myself was not sure if I'd be able to fulfill the job's requirements; however, the tools felt right and the work went well.

That night around the dinner table with him, his wife and three other employees, he said, "See that man?" pointing to me. "He learned his trade the way I learned, and you guys should watch how he holds his tools and works with them." With that comment, I relaxed, knowing that what I had learned in my trade had remained both in my mind and in my hands. This lifted my spirits and improved my view of the future.

Reunion

As time went on, Frank and I continued to inquire about the status of our emigration papers. We heard from George that he had moved from Brantford to Toronto and had a steady job working as a plastics mould designer. His steady employment enabled him to send visas to our parents in Hungary, allowing them to immigrate to Canada. Since my father had become a pensioner in 1955, the Communist Hungarian government gladly gave him an exit visa because they didn't sent payments to pensioners abroad.

Our emigration process was going much slower than predicted, and while we were still waiting, our parents' papers to emigrate from Hungary to Canada were already in progress. They finally left Hungary in April 1958, travelling on visas that would take them by train to Vienna, so they could visit us and fly from there to Toronto. Unbeknownst to the Hungarian authorities, we got permission from the Canadian consulate in Vienna for them stay with us for a month before continuing on their way. We had enough money saved to put them up in a hotel in Korneuburg and they spent the evenings in the camp with us after we got home from work.

We finally arrived in New York on December 29, 1958, and took the train from New York to Hartford, Connecticut, where Uncle Josef was waiting at the railway station. We spent about a week and a half with him and his wife, Ella, on their farm, enjoying their hospitality, though we disappointed our uncle by telling him we didn't want to stay and work on the farm with him. Our happiness in being with family again was surpassed only when, within a short while, we arrived in Toronto and visited our parents, George, Veronica and their little son, Alvin.

In Hartford, with our uncle's help, we found a rooming house and looked for jobs. We were both able to find work immediately. My landlord, who also owned a variety store, recommended me to a furniture frame company. I made one dollar an hour, which was good for the time, and I worked there for two months. Then I got a job repairing tobacco sheds, for which I was paid $1.50 an hour and given more hours. Sensing that I would lose my job in the off-season, I applied for a job as a skilled cabinetmaker and was hired. I made fine furniture from July 1959 to 1965. Something that I am very proud of can still be found in the Old State House in Hartford: I built a replica of the table the Declaration of Independence was signed on. It took me six months to build the half-circle table and thirteen matching chairs, all from solid mahogany with atlas and ebony wood inlays.

I had no problems integrating into American culture. I knew beforehand that I would have to adapt and I had a good social life. Of course, I was usually too busy with work to worry about much else. The life philosophy and attitude I had developed after the war, to always improve my mind, work hard and achieve my goals, helped tremendously to build a successful new life for myself on this side of the world.

Since I didn't speak the language or know the social customs of the country, within days I enrolled at night school for two or three nights a week of English as a second language classes. There was no social assistance for new immigrants to go to school as there is now in Canada, so it had to be night school. If you wanted to progress, you had to have the will and initiative to do it on your own.

My parents raised all three of us to be ambitious, hard-working people who wouldn't be satisfied with aiming at simple existence, but rather the kind who strives for more and is willing to work for it. I quickly jumped through the grades and in a year and a half graduated from Grade 4, but I then realized how much I still needed to learn to thrive in North America. After discussing my situation with one of my teachers, I enrolled in a two-year accounting certificate program. I studied, using a dictionary, and finished the course successfully. I worked hard because I hadn't left my life in Hungary, which I had already rebuilt after the concentration camp, just to have a job that provided the bare necessities. I had taken a big step in replanting myself on the other side of the ocean and would have to rebuild my life a third time, to achieve something better.

At Frank's wedding in Montreal in 1959, I met Eva, a very beautiful young woman born in Budapest. We fell in love and, in May 1961, we got married. Eva is also a Holocaust survivor. As a little girl, she lived with her mother in the Budapest ghetto as well as in protected houses, with papers supplied by Raoul Wallenberg, until their liberation.

Our two daughters, Judy and Edith, were born in 1963 and 1965, respectively. We decided that, although they would have to learn about our horrendous experiences, as they were growing up we would also teach them about the dangers of hatred and bigotry, that they should only hate ideas that spread discrimination and prejudice and which encourage people to not see others as equals. We succeeded and they don't tolerate any type of injustice around them.

Many survivors never speak of the horror-filled atrocities that they endured during the Holocaust. I, on the other hand, always spoke about my experiences to our children. It definitely influenced them in their desire for higher achievements, their willingness to work hard for their goals and their determination to appreciate and treat others as equals. With our guidance and subtle influence, they studied and worked hard. Judy is now a successful chartered accountant and Edith is a lawyer, both with their own families. According to the Nazi regime's plan to kill me and Eva, that five-year-old little girl in the Budapest ghetto, their generation should not have been born. Now, they live in a free country and enjoy a well-educated, balanced life, contributing to society's progress. It gives me and Eva immense pride that, while both our parents were from small towns and had a Grade 6 education, and we ourselves had only a high school and some college education, we raised university-educated children in defiance of all those odds.

In the early 1960s my father came up with the idea that his three sons should start some kind of a business together. We all liked this plan and after weighing the possibilities we decided to start a tool-and-die manufacturing shop in Toronto, specializing in moulds for the plastics industry. George, being a plastics mould designer, would do the sales and design; Frank, a tool-and-die maker, would lead the technical and manufacturing side; and I would manage the finances, purchasing and administration.

Frank and his family immigrated to Toronto in 1965, and my family and I immigrated in 1967; with that move, our original plan for our entire family to be together again finally became reality. All three of us put in a small, equal amount of savings, purchased the most basic machinery and started our shop. We called it FGL Precision Works and through connections in both of my brothers' workplaces, we got our first jobs. With good quality service, day and night, we slowly progressed. In the first few years we worked long hours seven days a week, sometimes working overnight to satisfy impatient customers. Many weeks went by without us taking home any salary, but with our determination to succeed we were moving ahead. As time passed, our shop grew, we hired more employees and we established a good name for ourselves in the industry.

In November 1972, disaster struck: my brother George was killed in an accident in our own plant when a gantry crane collapsed. We were devastated. It was a terrible tragedy and a painful memory that we have to live with. Nonetheless, we eventually had to continue working and soon reorganized our business. Frank took over sales and we had to hire some designers. Our good reputation, contacts and the loyalty of our customers allowed us to continue. We started to move toward computerized machinery in the mid-1980s and became a high-tech mould-manufacturing plant. In 1998, we decided to sell the business. We found the right buyer and concluded the sale. I stayed on for another year as a consultant and at age seventy-two – after working for fifty-eight years – I took full retirement.

By the end, our plant was employing forty people; the majority of shops in our industry employed only six to fifteen workers. I not only enjoyed the freedom, equality and respect that Canada provided me, but was also able to give something back, helping the country's growth by providing a livelihood for those forty families. I had reached my life-long goal of achieving something to be proud of.

～

One day in the late 1970s, my father called me and said that he read in the *Menorah*, Toronto's Hungarian-Jewish newspaper, that a Rebbetzin Jungreis would be speaking at the Shaarei Tefillah synagogue. "Is it possible that she is related to our beloved rabbi?" he said. "Would you come with me?" Naturally I said yes and when we arrived that Sunday afternoon, I asked one of the ushers if it would be possible to speak to the rebbetzin. His answer was no, absolutely not, her plane was late and there were 650 people waiting for her. I asked him to please just mention to her that a man from Nádudvar was there. She might ignore it, but we would just wait and see.

When she came down the stairs, the usher whispered to her and she almost stumbled, then looked around and rested her eyes on me. I approached her and told her who I was, that I was there with my father from Nádudvar, and that I was probably the last person to see her grandfather alive. She was the daughter of Avrom Jungreis, whose words were scratched into a cabinet in barracks F, block 11, at Bergen-Belsen. I told her – while the 650 people waited – how her grandfather, Yisrael, had blessed me before the cattle car's door was closed and chained in Strasshof. We spoke for about five minutes and when she went into the auditorium to deliver her speech, she incorporated my story into it, saying that she had just met me and through me had received a blessing after thirty-five years from her beloved grandfather.

She also said she was going to write about this meeting in her first soon-to-be published book, *The Jewish Soul on Fire*; she refers to the story in chapter 11, "Religious Dilemmas." On a subsequent visit to Toronto she gave me a copy of the book into which she wrote, "You have given me much inspiration in writing the chapter on religious dilemmas. May the almighty God who preserved your beautiful family from Nádudvar continue to watch over you and yours from generation to generation. May the Torah always continue in your wonderful family." I value this gift tremendously.

Esther Jungreis is the founder and head of the Hineni organization and is an outstanding orator who is very respected in high religious and political circles. She inherited her grandfather's oratorical skills – our esteemed rabbi had the ability to keep any audience spellbound. Between the two world wars, whenever a Hungarian government project was dedicated, there were always three religious leaders – one Protestant, one Roman Catholic and one Jewish – along with government representatives making the appropriate speeches. Whenever a project came up east of the Tisza River, our rabbi was asked to be the representative. The eloquence and clarity of his delivery, in perfect Hungarian, was uncommon.

~

In 2009, I heard about a project that had begun eight years earlier that led me to experience another incredible reunion from my past: I met some of the men who had liberated me back in 1945. It all started in a small village called Hudson Falls in New York State in 2001, when a high school history teacher named Matthew Rozell gave his students an assignment to interview family members who had fought in war. One of the students interviewed his grandfather, Carrol Walsh, a World War II veteran who became a Supreme Court judge. He spoke to his grandson about D-Day and beyond and how in April 1945, as tank commander, he and his men were heading toward Magdeburg, Germany. Mr. Rozell went back to further interview Mr. Walsh and toward the end of the interview, his daughter told her dad that he had forgotten to tell the story about the train. "What train?" his grandson asked. His grandfather told them that during one of their battles with the Germans, the division commander got word that there was an abandoned train about fifteen kilometres outside of Magdeburg and sent men in two tanks and a jeep to investigate. On that train the men found 2,500 emaciated Holocaust survivors. I was one of them. The "death train" they later called it.

After the interview, Mr. Rozell went home and began to do some research, including interviewing another member of the Ninth Army, a tank driver named George Gross, who had taken photos on that fateful day. He was then able to connect with Frank Towers, the liaison officer who had provided quarters in Hillersleben for us survivors the day after liberation. Matthew Rozell wrote a blog entry about this incredible story on the school's website in 2002 that was noticed by a survivor of the train in 2004. When the Associated Press got wind of the story, more and more people heard about it. In 2007, some of the liberators were located and held a reunion in South Carolina and in September 2009, I learned by chance that they were going to hold another reunion, this time uniting liberators with survivors. I had been at a meeting with Paul Arato, a business acquaintance, and as we spoke, realizing we were both from the same area in Hungary, we asked each other about our past. Amazingly, we discovered we had both been in the same block at Bergen-Belsen and on that fateful train as well, and it was he who had happened upon the reunion information.

At the symposium, seven liberators and seven survivors met for the first time since that day in April 1945. Almost sixty-five years later,

I met the men who gave me back my life! It was a miracle that I had never dreamed could happen. I spoke at one of the six different sessions at the symposium, which was attended by about four hundred students from the surrounding area, and I also spoke with the liberating veterans, whom I call "the angels of my life." Both CBS and ABC News picked up the story, and when I was interviewed by someone from ABC, it was broadcast around the world – everywhere, I heard, except Canada. All seven of us survivors became honorary members of the 30th Infantry Division – the Old Hickory division they call it – of the American army. Frank Towers was president of the 30th division at the time, and signed the honorary certificate I have.

I kept in touch with both Carrol Walsh and Frank Towers and their families, and our mutual love and respect continue to keep us connected. I attended the last symposium in 2011 and that November, Eva and I visited Mr. Walsh in Florida, where we spend the winters. In December 2012, I spoke to him the day before he passed away. Eva and I, our two daughters, and our granddaughter Jessica attended Mr. Walsh's military funeral in Johnstown, New York, in July 2013 and Jessica honoured him during the March of the Living when she marched in both Eva's and my honour as well as in his memory.

Epilogue

Educating students about the Holocaust is extremely important to me. I've spoken at dozens of schools and have been a keynote speaker for Yom HaShoah, Holocaust Remembrance Day, in Ottawa and in Sydney, Nova Scotia. In 2010, I was one of eighteen Holocaust survivors honoured at Queen's Park in Toronto by Yad Vashem and the premier of Ontario for my contribution, through my business, to the progress of Ontario and for my commitment to Holocaust education.

I am very involved in the Toronto Holocaust Centre's educational program and a number of years ago I had the honour of being included among their distinguished list, displayed on their walls, of "We who survived." The centre brings in thousands of high school students from Toronto and the surrounding area who are learning about the Holocaust as part of their history courses. They see an exhibit, watch a documentary film and then listen to a Holocaust survivor tell his or her story.

I speak at the centre because always, in every group, quite a number of students send letters in which they tell me that I made an indelible impression on them and that they will try to be better people after hearing my experiences. Many times, I am also asked why I relive the horrors in my mind. I tell them that through their letters, I can see that many of them are looking at things differently than they did before. They understand, through my experiences, what prejudice, discrimination, hatred and injustice can lead to, and hopefully they

– one person, one day at a time – will fight against it. That knowledge is my payment and reward, and I will continue to speak as long as I am able to. I also paraphrase a quote from Nobel Laureate Elie Wiesel, that I tell my story to the next generation so my past will not become their future. I don't enjoy reliving my experiences, but people who were fortunate enough to have lived life without going through the Holocaust, and the new generations growing up, have to be told about it so they can help prevent it from being repeated for any person, group or nation.

I always tell the students that they need to remember that every survivor's story is different and unique. To have not succumbed to the death that took so many, everyone who survived lived from one day to the next through a series of miracles and acts of fate. I am very frequently asked, "What kept you going in those horrific circumstances?" My answer is a simple, four-letter word: hope. Hope to survive the day and wake up alive the next and live that day through, too.

Another thing I cannot emphasize enough is that the atrocities we endured and through which six million of our brethren lost their lives is the result of another single word that ruled sick minds: hatred. This word has never had a place in my mind and my life. I have never hated anyone or any group of people because they are in some way different from me. Hatred is such an evil aspect of human life that consumes the hater; that person loses everything decent and good and lives life only for hatred. Hatred can start first with verbal abuse or even with just a mild joke about some individual or group, but it can accelerate to beating and then killing the oppressed; the Holocaust is an unparalleled example in history. Tragically, we are again experiencing an unprecedented level of hatred around the globe by people who live their lives for the purpose of destroying others. In this global atmosphere it is even more important to do the utmost to teach and influence the younger generations to fight against those horrific trends.

Eva Meisels' Memoir

I was born in Budapest, Hungary on July 3, 1939. My parents, Erno and Irene (née Goldner) Silber, were married on August 14, 1938. My mother, the eldest of nine children, was from the small town of Ibrány in the province of Szabolcs. My father, who was born in Komádi, in Bihar province, had four brothers and a sister. My mother told me that after my birth, my grandmothers took turns coming to Budapest to help her out, each for two weeks at a time.

Both my maternal and paternal grandparents were Orthodox and quite religious, neither poor nor rich, and both had a store and a small workshop to make the merchandise they sold. My maternal grandparents, Juliska and Adolf, made cabinets and my paternal grandparents worked with sheet metal. In 1942, before the war came to Hungary, I visited them both, staying with each for a short while. In the photo I still have of that time, my mother is the only one who has her hair covered – which was customary in the Orthodox Jewish way of life – because she was the only one who was married. My father, however, was in a forced labour camp then, so he is not in the picture.

When my father was sixteen or so, he and two of his brothers joined their father in the sheet metal trade. They travelled from town to town and worked for different people, learning more details of their trade. My mom worked in a grocery store until I was born and my parents lived with some of my aunts in a small apartment in Budapest to save money until we found our own place in the seventh district on Klauzál tér 15. Our apartment was on the second floor, number 20.

My father worked in Budapest during the late 1930s and early 1940s, until the anti-Jewish laws came into effect and Jews couldn't work in certain professions. From then on, he took whatever job was available, even shovelling snow for the municipality. In 1942, he was called up for forced labour. That year, he was allowed to come home for a day once because Mom was able to get a telegram to him that I was terribly sick and that she didn't know if I was going to make it. At some point over the next three years, he worked the mines in Bor, Yugoslavia, eventually ending up in the Mauthausen concentration camp. He was liberated by the Americans in May 1945, but he didn't make it home until August.

I hadn't seen my father for a number of years and the day he came home was something that I'll never forget. My mother was out, buying old clothes that she would then wash and mend to re-sell, and my father's great-aunt was looking after me. My great-aunt and I were sitting outside our building as a man came toward us. When this stranger saw me, he started running, calling out my name. He was crying and laughing at the same time that he was hugging me. I'm not even sure that I knew who he was. I heard my great-aunt tell him that my mother was well and that she was out, and then he asked questions about the other members of our family – who was home and who was not. Many of our relatives had been taken during the war and never returned.

I was told that my father's sister, Yitte Brandle, was deported with a load of other young girls in Budapest. As she was boarding the train, she decided she wouldn't go. According to witnesses, she tried to run away and was shot. She was my father's only sister. I named my daughter after her.

When I visited my uncle Bela, who has since passed away, in Detroit after the war, he told me stories about the family that I hadn't ever heard before. He knew that around Passover of 1944, my grandmother's neighbour, a kind gentile lady, came to Budapest and was supposed to take me with her to the countryside. My maternal grandparents thought that I would be safer there than I would be in Budapest. But my mother didn't let me go; she thought that we should stay together and whatever happened to her would happen to me too. Three weeks later, my grandparents and my three younger aunts and uncles were deported to Auschwitz and murdered there. I cannot imagine the agony my mother had to go through in those few hours to make that life-altering decision, not knowing what the future would bring.

Mom and I ended up in the Budapest ghetto, which included our house in Klauzál tér. I can remember certain things from that time, and others I heard from my mother as I was growing up. When more and more people started moving into our building, I had no idea it was the ghetto – I only noticed that things were changing. What does a four- or five-year-old know about politics or hate?

By this time, we were wearing the yellow star on our clothing, according to a law that had been enforced a few weeks after the Nazi occupation on March 19, 1944. My mother took it off me once and ex-plained how to leave our building and get to the nearby small market. There, I had to look amongst the stalls for our former neighbour. I saw her at a counter and when she noticed me, she reached down behind the counter and gave me some bread to take home to my mother. She must have liked us and cared about us, to risk being caught and punished for giving bread to a Jewish girl. She certainly didn't want anyone to know I was Jewish. I had no right being out without the yellow star and if anyone had recognized me and turned me in, that would have been the end of both of us. I don't think I knew then what it meant for my mother to have the courage to let her little girl go outside, not knowing if she was going to make it back safely.

In the ghetto, there were three houses on each side of the main square. We lived in the middle one and some people tried to find an underground route through our basement in case we ever had to escape. When they pulled down some walls to the next building, they found a hidden storage of goose liver. The Jewish man who had lived there was a manufacturer and before he was taken away, he had stored all the supplies he had behind a fake wall. We had no bread, so it was very greasy and nobody was very well after eating it, but for about three weeks that was the only food we had. I still love goose liver today.

I can remember seeing the dead bodies piled up in the middle of the main square where the sandbox used to be. About ten years later, when I saw bodies on the street again during the revolution against the Communist regime, I felt immune to it, as if it didn't even affect me.

Twice, we were ordered to leave our apartment and go downstairs to the courtyard. I don't know whether it was the Arrow Cross or the SS who came to our building. My mother held me in her arms amid the commotion – noise, yelling, crying – and I started to scream; a man told my mother to get away from him with that screaming child. He couldn't handle the noise, which might have saved us. A number of people were taken away and they never came back. A few days later, they came back but this time I didn't cry. I took it all in, perhaps out of interest, until my mother pinched my behind and I started to scream again. Luckily, the same thing happened and we were asked to leave.

One day, we didn't manage to get away and were marched all along the banks of the Danube. We had no idea where they were taking us. People who were not going fast enough or didn't do exactly what they were ordered to do were shot. I saw bodies falling into the river, sometimes bodies that had been tied together, so that only one bullet had to be used.

I don't know whether it was then or later on that we were taken to a place was called Nyilas House and all I can remember was a great huge grey blanket on the ground, maybe more than one, and everybody had to put all their valuables on them. I still remember seeing my mother pulling off her wedding band and throwing it down on that blanket.

My mother, great-aunt and I stood in the Nyilas House from morning to night, facing the wall. Between the three of us we had only an apple. My great-aunt told me to eat it because I was hungry; I don't remember this, but my mother told me that I said that I wasn't going to eat it because who knows if we were going to have food tomorrow. I don't know if I did that because I was smart or stupid, or if it was just that I was a little child who had experienced a lot and come to a logical conclusion. Late that night, we were ordered back to the ghetto.

The Nyilas incident happened about the time that a distant relative managed to get hold of some false papers for us from Raoul Wallenberg, a Swedish diplomat. My mom, aunt and I had everything we owned in a wheelbarrow – from where we got it I haven't the faintest idea – and we managed to get to a safe house. The safe house was close by, right outside of the ghetto on Akácfa utca 26.

By the time we ended up there it was a bitterly cold winter and I remember a lot of people being in the home. I also remember trying to get hold of some water, not so much to bathe – for which we used snow – but at least to drink, and the faucets were down in the courtyard; we had to stand in line with everybody else to get our water, which was barely dripping because it was frozen. I collected the water in a pot as it dripped down. I don't know how we managed to get food in those days but we didn't starve. My mother later told me that sometimes she soaked dry bread crusts in the snow.

When we moved down to a bomb shelter in the basement, my mother took turns with the other women going upstairs to cook food for the children and everybody downstairs. They used a Jewish man's apartment because his kitchen still had a few supplies. Once, a bomb fell on our building while my mother was up there. She ran downstairs and when she saw that I was all right, she covered me with her body, just yelling and screaming. Her hair was white and I thought it had suddenly turned white but it was the dust from the building.

Many times, people ask me what we did, as little children, in a basement all day long. My mother made a doll for me from a sock, which she drew a little face on, and my friends and I played with it.

We were liberated by the Soviet army in January 1945. They were going from house to house looking for Nazis hiding in civilian clothes. When we saw men coming down the basement stairs with guns bigger than a soldier, pointing it ahead of them because they didn't know what they were going to face, I didn't know who they were or what was going on. They spoke a different language – I probably couldn't distinguish between German and Russian. One young soldier came over to the corner where I was huddled together with other children; in one hand he had a huge rifle or gun and with the other he reached back into his knapsack and took out some dark brown bread and handed it to us. I will remember that dark bread as long as I live. It was something we hadn't seen in a long time and the fact that it was coming from a person who was also holding a gun had an effect on me.

When we finally came out of the basement, I couldn't see. My mother told me that for three or four days I simply could not see at all. My eyes weren't accustomed to the light and she would tell me to keep my eyes closed and just open them for a few minutes each time, a little bit longer each day, until I got used to the daylight again.

When the basement was again used for storing coal and wood after liberation, I was always afraid to go back down there because I knew in what corner a neighbour had died or where somebody else had passed away from starvation. If I had to go down there, I went singing and whistling and my parents may have thought I was crazy for being afraid of the shadows from the memories.

⌒

After the war, we were able to recover some of our possessions. When my maternal grandparents had been ordered to move into the ghetto, their trusted friend, Kato Antal, came over the night before and he told them that he would try to help them save whatever they wanted.

I was told later on that he gathered jewellery, photographs, furniture and even religious items. He buried everything in his own backyard and gave it back to members of our family who returned. My parents got back some family photos and my grandfather's gold pocket-watch chain. My father, who worked for a year as a jeweller, made three little bracelets out of it for my mother and two of her sisters. I lost my mother's and I feel guilty about it even today, not because of its monetary value but because of the memories and that it was my grandfather's. Kato Antal also helped my grandparents by bringing them food while they were in the ghetto. We were so thankful to him for everything he did. My uncles, who live in the United States, helped him and his family however they could after the war.

Following liberation, everybody listened for news, stopping people on the streets and asking, "Where were you? Did you see so and so?", hoping to hear something about their loved ones. My mother and I travelled to Ibrány, my mother's hometown, which took us three days instead of the usual three or four hours because everything was so disorganized. While we were there, my uncle Bela (Ben) and my mom heard a rumour that one of my aunts, Bözsi (Elisabeth), was alive in Romania. My mother left me with my uncle and travelled by train to Romania to look for her sister; it took her about a week to get there and back. By that time, my aunt had been liberated by the Americans, but the Soviets had taken her to the Soviet Union. My father's brother was also captured by the Soviets but they never met up there. Neither of them was able to get back until 1947. When my aunt arrived home it was early in the morning, I was in bed, and I remember her kissing me as her tears ran over me.

My mother lost four siblings and my father lost two. My family members who made it back to Hungary were still hoping that some of our other relatives were alive and they all came to our home because they knew people would reunite there. My aunt Olga, who we had heard was killed, came home! I was with my mother and we heard someone yelling and screaming my mother's name and when we looked outside in the courtyard we saw my aunt, whom we called Tiny because she was a very short lady. My mom ran down the stairs and Tiny ran up and they met up in front of an apartment. After everything they had gone through, they were crying freely. Everyone around them was so emotional and happy until a man opened his apartment door and started to yell at my mother to be quiet because he couldn't sleep with noise like that. Can you imagine?

My paternal grandmother, Margaret, survived Auschwitz. When she made her way back to Hungary, she found out that my grandfather had perished. The first time she told me stories about the family in detail was when we decided to leave Hungary after the 1956 revolution. She wouldn't escape with us because we were the first ones in our family to leave the country and she was waiting until my other aunts and uncles could leave; she followed later on. The night before we left, when she came and stayed over at our home, she started telling me a lot of stories about the war.

My grandmother Margaret lived in Montreal until she passed away in 2001 at the age of 102. She used to come to Toronto once or twice a year as long as she was able, and when she couldn't do it any longer, I went to Montreal to stay with her. We would talk half the night away while she recalled her memories. She was a wonderful lady, ultra-Orthodox her whole life, who survived Auschwitz on potato skins and rotten vegetables; she wouldn't eat any of what they called soup because she didn't know what was in it and she wouldn't touch it if it wasn't kosher. She still survived.

~

Before the war, I went to a Jewish nursery school and I still have a picture of a Chanukah party there with all my little girlfriends. I was with these friends in the ghetto basement. After the war, my parents sent me to a Jewish elementary school. The school existed until I had just about finished Grade 4, after which, under communism, all the schools became nationalized. Then I went to the regular elementary school in the public school system, followed by high school.

My father had changed our last name to Sugar. He had been thinking of going into the police force to hunt for Nazis, and felt that the name sounded more Hungarian. He didn't end up in the force, but was quite active in a Zionist movement, helping a number of Jews get to Israel. In 1945, 1946 and even in 1947, it was very difficult to get out of Hungary. My father helped people travel by finding them connections and places to stay.

Once, some people came to our home when I was alone and my dad was at work and asked me questions about my father, about whether I had seen a certain person lately and if my father ever came home late, alone or with others. Now that I think back, it seems they wanted information on whether my dad had helped people get out of the country. I was only eight or nine years old and to every question I said, "I don't know," but they waited and waited. They were there for quite a while and when my father came home he managed to talk his way out of it. He didn't get into any kind of trouble. He told me that I had been very smart to answer "I don't know" to every question.

Life eventually started to normalize. My parents worked and I was in school. Then, in October 1956, the revolution hit. There was a shortage of food once again. We had to stand in line to try to get bread and sometimes when we were close to the beginning of a line, Soviet tanks would appear and start to shoot. We all scattered and many people were shot. There were dead bodies on the streets of Budapest again.

We started to hear rumours about paying people off to get across the border to Austria and freedom, so on December 9, 1956, my parents and I, wearing as many layers of clothing as we could, left everything else behind and walked to the Eastern Railway station in Budapest. We were being smuggled out with a group of people and as we walked toward Andau, Austria, we hid from the constant flare of searchlights. In our group, there was a small child who was given a sleeping pill so that her crying would not give us away. Tragically, she died before we reached freedom.

When we made it to Vienna, we met up with an acquaintance of my mother's and slept at his shop, on top of piles of textiles. The next day, we went to the Hebrew Immigrant Aid Society and as we stood in line, we heard someone yelling my mother's name. A man approached, someone she didn't recognize at first because she hadn't seen him in ten years…it was her brother Bela! He had heard about the revolution and had travelled from Detroit in the hopes of finding our family and helping us get out. From that moment on, we had a place to stay, food and warm clothing. I ate my first-ever clementine and when my uncle asked me what else I'd like, the first thing that came to mind was "Coca-Cola." I'd heard about it but had never tried one. That was the first and last time I drank a cola – I hated it!

We had hoped to immigrate to the US, but the American consulate said we'd be waiting a long time, so we decided to immigrate to Canada where my dad's younger brother lived. He had made his way to Paris right after liberation and from there to Quebec. We stayed in Vienna for a few days and then left from Bremerhaven on the SS *Berlin* luxury liner near the end of December, arriving at Pier 21 in Halifax on January 9, 1957. The Canadian government wanted to send us to Saskatchewan to be farmers, but my mother argued with the translator they sent, saying we had family in Montreal. Eventually, my mother showed the translator a letter, which she could not read because she only spoke Hungarian, so my mom told her that the letter stated they had both jobs and family waiting in Montreal. It didn't actually say that at all, but it worked.

Finally, Montreal became our new home. I continued my schooling at Sir George Williams College. We all started to work and to go to night school to learn English and try to establish ourselves. We moved to Windsor for a short time because my father couldn't find work in Montreal, but then we moved back. I worked in the IBM service bureau as a billing clerk.

In 1959 I was invited to a wedding where I met my husband, Leslie. We got married on May 28, 1961 and lived in Hartford, Connecticut for six years and started our family; then we moved to Toronto to be with his family and start our own business. Through the North York Board of Education, I began working with physically and mentally challenged children. During this time, I continued taking courses at Seneca College and York University.

We always talked about our past to our children and they speak Hungarian because we wanted them to be able to communicate with their grandparents. In 1991, our daughter Judy, who became a chartered accountant, had an opportunity to go to Hungary and work there implementing Western-style accounting methods. She was there for three months and it helped a lot to be able to speak the language. Our other daughter, Edith, had finished law school and, while she was waiting to take the bar exam, she travelled to Hungary as well, so my husband and I decided it was time to go back and see what it was like there.

Aside from one pleasant visit to Nádudvar, where we drove to Leslie's parents' old place and ate apricots from the tree his mother had planted, I had a terrible impression of the country. All I can say is that I'm sorry that we still have some relatives there and that there are still a number of Jews there, but otherwise I couldn't care less what happens to Hungary. I have too many bad memories and I don't think anything has changed. The antisemitism is just as bad as it was before. I saw carvings on public benches that said, "We'll take care of our own Jews. You don't need to take them as far as Auschwitz." I saw it. And, just walking down the street, I heard drunks making antisemitic remarks. My cousin sent his children to a Jewish school and stones were thrown at them on their first day there. In the synagogue where my grandmother used to go, I saw the windows broken – the same windows that I had seen broken in 1956. The Dohany shul, where we belonged, is the exception. It is the second-largest synagogue in Europe and is still really gorgeous; it was beautifully renovated. Shortly after liberation, a memorial was erected there for people who perished in the Holocaust and my parents had our family members' names engraved on it.

~

In 1996, I attended the unveiling of the Raoul Wallenberg statue in Earl Bales Park and seventeen years later, I was honoured to unveil the new Canadian postage stamp that bears his photo. Our four beautiful grandchildren, Jessica, Rachel, Jordan and Jaimee, know about our past and have attended various Holocaust education events. When our oldest granddaughter, Jessica, was preparing for her bat mitzvah she took part in the Holocaust Centre of Toronto's twinning program, which helps youth remember and learn about their family history. Jessica dedicated her bat mitzvah to my aunt Ella, who was eleven years old when she was taken to Auschwitz and never had a chance to have one. Rachel dedicated hers to Leslie's cousin Jimmy Groszman, who was also eleven when he was killed by the Nazis.

There are too many names of loved ones we lost in the war. This is what I remember. Having a normal life – children and grandchildren – was not what Hitler had in mind for the Jews. No matter what age we were, we cannot forget the Holocaust. It's part of my life. Maybe it would be nice to forget, but if we did, then others who never heard of these atrocities will not know, and it would be much easier to repeat in the future. This is why my husband and I are active in Holocaust education both in Toronto and Florida. We feel that it is important for youth, especially, to hear about our past so that it does not become their future.

Glossary

Allied Zones of Germany The four zones that Germany was divided into after its defeat in World War II, each administered by one of the four major Allied powers – the United States, Britain, France and the Soviet Union. These administrative zones existed in Germany between 1945 and 1949.

American Jewish Joint Distribution Committee (JDC) Also known colloquially as the "Joint." A charitable organization that provided material support for persecuted Jews in Germany and other Nazi-occupied territories and facilitated their emigration to neutral countries such as Portugal, Turkey and China. Between 1939 and 1944, JDC officials helped close to 81,000 European Jews find asylum in various parts of the world. Between 1944 and 1947, the JDC assisted more than 100,000 refugees living in DP camps by offering retraining programs, cultural activities and financial assistance for emigration.

antisemitism Prejudice, discrimination, persecution and/or hatred against Jewish people, institutions, culture and symbols.

Appell (German) Roll call.

Arrow Cross (in Hungarian, Nyilaskeresztes Párt – Hungarista Mozgalom; abbreviation: Nyilas) A Hungarian nationalistic and antisemitic party founded by Ferenc Szálasi in 1935 under the name the Party of National Will. With the full support of Nazi

Germany, the newly renamed Arrow Cross Party ran in Hungary's 1939 election and won 25 per cent of the vote. The party was banned shortly after the elections, but was legalized again in March 1944 when Germany occupied Hungary. Under Nazi approval, the party assumed control of Hungary from October 15, 1944, to March 1945, led by Szálasi under the name the Government of National Unity. The Arrow Cross regime was particularly brutal toward Jews – in addition to the thousands of Hungarian Jews who had been deported to Nazi death camps during the previous Miklós Horthy regime, the Arrow Cross, during their short period of rule, instigated the murder of tens of thousands of Hungarian Jews. Between December 1944 and January 1945, the Arrow Cross murdered approximately 20,000 Jews, many of whom had been forced into a closed ghetto at the end of November 1944.

Auschwitz (German; in Polish, Oświęcim) A town in southern Poland approximately forty kilometres from Krakow, it is also the name of the largest complex of Nazi concentration camps that were built nearby. The Auschwitz complex contained three main camps: Auschwitz I, a slave labour camp built in May 1940; Auschwitz II-Birkenau, a death camp built in early 1942; and Auschwitz-Monowitz, a slave labour camp built in October 1942. In 1941, Auschwitz I was a testing site for usage of the lethal gas Zyklon B as a method of mass killing, which then went into wide usage. Between 1942 and 1944, transports arrived at Auschwitz-Birkenau from almost every country in Europe – hundreds of thousands from both Poland and Hungary, and thousands from France, the Netherlands, Greece, Slovakia, Bohemia and Moravia, Yugoslavia, Belgium, Italy and Norway. As well, more than thirty thousand people were deported there from other concentration camps. Between May 15 and July 8, 1944, approximately 435,000 Hungarian Jews were deported to Auschwitz. It is estimated that 1.1 million people were murdered in Auschwitz; approximately 950,000 were Jewish; 74,000 Polish; 21,000 Roma; 15,000 Soviet prisoners of war; and 10,000-15,000 other nationalities. The Auschwitz complex was liberated by the Soviet army in January 1945.

Austro-Hungarian Empire Also known as the Dual Monarchy of Austria and Hungary, ruled by the royal Habsburg family. It was successor to the Austrian Empire (1804–1867) and functioned as a dual-union state in Central Europe from 1867 to 1918. A multinational empire, the Dual Monarchy was notable for the constant political and ethnic disputes among its eleven principal national groups. Although the Empire adopted a Law of Nationalities, which officially accorded language and cultural rights to various ethnic groups, in practice there were many inequalities in how the groups were treated. Jews were granted both citizenship rights and equal status to other minority groups but minorities such as the Slovaks, for example, were excluded from the political sphere, whereas Czechs were accepted into government positions. The Austro-Hungarian Empire dissolved at the end of World War I and divided into the separate and independent countries of Austria, Hungary and Czechoslovakia.

bar mitzvah, bat mitzvah (Hebrew; literally, one to whom commandments apply) The age of thirteen when, according to Jewish tradition, boys become religiously and morally responsible for their actions and are considered adults for the purpose of synagogue ritual. A bar mitzvah is also the synagogue ceremony and family celebration that mark the attainment of this status, during which the boy is called upon to read a portion of the Torah and recite the prescribed prayers in a public prayer forum. In the latter half of the twentieth century, liberal Jews instituted an equivalent ceremony and celebration for girls called a bat mitzvah.

Becher, Kurt (1909–1995) SS lieutenant and colonel who was the commissar of concentration camps in Germany and also held the position of Chief of the Economic Department of the SS Command in Hungary after the 1944 German occupation. As economic chief, he led negotiations on behalf of SS authorities

Heinrich Himmler and Adolf Eichmann with Jewish representatives to extort wealth from Jews in exchange for saving the lives of some, in what became known as "Kasztner's train," which led to the survival of about one thousand Jews, as well as the "Jews on ice" deal, which led to the deportation of approximately 20,000 Jews to labour camps in Austria, where many survived. After the war, Becher was not tried as a war criminal due to Rudolf (Rezső) Kasztner's testimony on his behalf. *See also* Kasztner, Rudolf.

Bergen-Belsen A camp initially established by the Nazis in 1940 for prisoners of war near Celle, Germany. After 1943, it held so-called exchange Jews in the "residence camp" and "star camp" whom Germany hoped to use in peace negotiations with the Allies, as well as to trade for German nationals. By December 1944, Bergen-Belsen was designated a concentration camp and its subcamps included one for prisoners-of-war; one for "neutrals" (citizens of neutral countries); a *Häftlingslager* (prisoners' camp); and an *Ungarnlager* (Hungarian camp) or *Sonderlager* (special camp) that held about 4,000 Jews to be potentially exchanged for money and other goods. Toward the end of the war, thousands of prisoners from camps close to the front lines, such as Auschwitz, Mittelbau-Dora and Buchenwald were taken to Bergen-Belsen, as were forced labourers from Hungary. With the influx of inmates, camp conditions deteriorated rapidly and some 35,000 people died between January and April 1945. British forces liberated the camp on April 15, 1945.

Budapest ghetto The area established by the government of Hungary on November 29, 1944. By December 10, the ghetto and its 33,000 Jewish inhabitants were sealed off from the rest of the city. At the end of December, Jews who had previously held "protected" status (many by the Swedish government) were moved into the ghetto and the number of residents increased to 55,000; by January 1945, the number had reached 70,000. The ghetto was overcrowded and lacked sufficient food, water and sanitation. Supplies dwindled and conditions worsened during the Soviet siege of Budapest and thousands died of starvation and disease. Soviet forces liberated the ghetto on January 18, 1945.

chalutzim (Hebrew; pioneers) A term used within Zionist youth movements outside of Palestine to refer to its members who hoped to immigrate there. *Chalutzim* were also agricultural immigrants who moved to pre-state Israel to establish settlements and build self-sustaining communities, primarily associated with the wave of immigration known as the Third Aliyah (1919–1923) that followed in the wake of World War I and the establishment of the British Mandate in Palestine.

Chanukah (also Hanukah; Hebrew; dedication) An eight-day festival celebrated in December to mark the victory of the Jews against foreign conquerors who desecrated the Temple in Jerusalem in the second century BCE. Traditionally, each night of the festival is marked by lighting an eight-branch candelabrum called a menorah to commemorate the rededication of the Temple and the miracle of its lamp burning for eight days without oil.

cheder (Hebrew; literally, room) An Orthodox Jewish elementary school that teaches the fundamentals of Jewish religious observance and textual study, as well as the Hebrew language.

Chumash (Hebrew) The Pentateuch. The term used to refer to the Five Books of Moses when they are in book form, as distinct from the Torah scrolls.

Eichmann, Adolf (1906–1962) The head of the Gestapo department responsible for the implementation of the Nazis' policy of mass murder of Jews (the so-called Final Solution), Eichmann was in charge of transporting Jews to death camps in Poland. In 1942, Eichmann coordinated deportations of Jewish populations from Slovakia, the Netherlands, France and Belgium. In 1944, he was directly involved in the deportations of Jews from Hungary, as well as in negotiations with Rudolf Kasztner to supply Jews for slave labour in Austria. After the war, Eichmann escaped from US custody and fled to Argentina, where he was captured in 1960 by Israeli intelligence operatives; his ensuing 1961 trial in Israel was widely and internationally televised. Eichmann was sentenced to death and hanged in May 1962.

ghetto A confined residential area for Jews. The term originated in Venice, Italy in 1516 with a law requiring all Jews to live on a segregated, gated island known as Ghetto Nuovo. Throughout the Middle Ages in Europe, Jews were often forcibly confined to gated Jewish neighbourhoods. During the Holocaust, the Nazis forced Jews to live in crowded and unsanitary conditions in rundown districts of cities and towns.

Häftling (German) Prison inmate.

Hebrew Immigrant Aid Society (HIAS) An organization founded in New York in 1881 that continues to provides aid, counsel, support and general assistance to Jewish immigrants all over the world. Since the early 1970s, HIAS has been especially active in providing assistance to Jews emigrating from the USSR.

high holidays (also High Holy Days) The autumn holidays that mark the beginning of the Jewish year and that include Rosh Hashanah (New Year) and Yom Kippur (Day of Atonement). Rosh Hashanah is observed with synagogue services where the leader of the service blows the shofar (ram's horn), and festive meals where sweet foods, such as apples and honey, are eaten to symbolize and celebrate a sweet new year. Yom Kippur, a day of fasting and prayer at synagogue, follows ten days later.

Hineni A Jewish organization and movement established in New York in 1989 by rebbetzin Esther Jungreis, which now has international branches. Jungreis, a Torah scholar, writer and public speaker, embraces the Torah as spiritual guidance and aims to educate Jews about Judaism.

Hungarian Revolution (1956) A spontaneous uprising against the Soviet-backed Communist government of Hungary in October 1956, the Hungarian Revolution led to the brief establishment of a reformist government under Prime Minister Imre Nagy. The revolution was swiftly crushed by the Soviet invasion of November 1956, during which thousands of civilians were killed.

Josef, Franz (1830–1916) Ruler of the Austro-Hungarian Empire from 1848–1916.

Kasztner, Rudolf (also, Kastner, Rezső) (1906–1957) Head of the Budapest Relief and Rescue Committee during WWII and infamous for his part in the "blood for trucks" negotiations with Adolf Eichmann that led to what became known as "Kasztner's train" – the release of 1,684 prominent Hungarian Jews to the neutral country of Switzerland in 1944. After the war, Kasztner's role in the negotiations was highly controversial: some viewed him as a collaborator while others applauded him for saving as many lives as he could under the circumstances. Kasztner was assassinated in Israel in 1957 after a widely publicized libel trial whose purpose had been to defend accusations against him but instead turned into a moral, politicized examination of his actions during the war. Although most of the guilty verdict was overturned in 1958, the original judge's oft-quoted ruling, that Kasztner "sold his soul to the devil," is still the subject of much debate.

kosher (Hebrew) Fit to eat according to Jewish dietary laws. Observant Jews follow a system of rules known as *kashruth* that regulates what can be eaten, how food is prepared and how meat and poultry are slaughtered. Food is kosher when it has been deemed fit for consumption according to this system of rules. There are several foods that are forbidden, most notably pork products and shellfish.

March of the Living An annual event that was established in 1988 and takes place in April on Holocaust Memorial Day (Yom Ha-Shoah) in Poland. The March of the Living program aims to educate primarily Jewish students and young adults from around the world about the Holocaust and Jewish life during World War II. Along with Holocaust survivors, participants march the three kilometres from Auschwitz to Birkenau to commemorate all who perished in the Holocaust. The concept of the event comes from the Nazi death marches that Jews were forced to go on when they were being evacuated from the forced labour and concentration camps at the very end of the war. Many Jews died during these marches and thus the March of the Living was created both to remember this history and to serve as a contrast to it by celebrating Jewish life and strength. After spending time in Poland, participants travel to Israel and join in celebrations there for Israel's remembrance and independence days.

Mauthausen A notoriously brutal Nazi concentration camp located about twenty kilometres east of the Austrian city of Linz. First established in 1936 shortly after the annexation of Austria to imprison "asocial" political opponents of the Third Reich, the camp grew to encompass fifty nearby subcamps and became the largest forced labour complex in the German-occupied territories. By the end of the war, close to 200,000 prisoners had passed through the Mauthausen forced labour camp system and almost 120,000 of them died there – including 38,120 Jews – from starvation, disease and hard labour. Mauthausen was classified as a Category 3 camp, which indicated the harshest conditions, and inmates were often worked to death in the brutal Weiner-Graben stone quarry. The US army liberated the camp on May 5, 1945.

mezuzah (Hebrew; literally, doorpost) The small piece of parchment inscribed with specific Hebrew texts from the Torah – usually enclosed in a decorative casing – that is placed on the door frames of homes of observant Jews.

minyan (Hebrew) The quorum of ten adult male Jews required for certain religious rites. The term can also designate a congregation.

motzi (abbreviation of *HaMotzi*; Hebrew, who brings forth) The beginning of the blessing recited over bread before a meal.

Nazi camps The Nazis established roughly 20,000 prison camps between 1933 and 1945. Although the term concentration camp is often used to refer generally to all these facilities, the various camps in fact served a wide variety of functions. They included concentration camps; forced labour camps; prisoner-of-war (POW) camps; transit camps; and death camps. Concentration camps were detention facilities first built in 1933 to imprison "enemies of the state," while forced labour camps held prisoners who had to do hard physical labour under brutal working conditions. POW camps were designated for captured prisoners of war and transit camps operated as holding facilities for Jews who were to be transported to main camps – often death camps in Poland. Death camps were killing centres where designated groups of people were murdered on a highly organized, mass scale. Some camps, such as Mauthausen, combined several of these functions into a huge complex of camps.

Orthodox The set of beliefs and practices of Jews for whom the observance of Jewish law is closely connected to faith; it is characterized by strict religious observance of Jewish dietary laws, restrictions on work on the Sabbath and holidays, and a modest code of dress.

Passover One of the major festivals of the Jewish calendar, Passover takes place over eight days in the spring. One of the main observances of the holiday is to recount the story of Exodus, the Jews' flight from slavery in Egypt, at a ritual meal called a seder. The name itself refers to the fact that God "passed over" the houses of the Jews when he set about slaying the firstborn sons of Egypt as the last of the ten plagues aimed at convincing Pharaoh to free the Jews.

Ravensbrück The largest Nazi concentration camp created almost exclusively for women that was established in May 1939 and located about ninety kilometres north of Berlin. Throughout the war, subcamps were built in the area around Ravensbrück to serve as forced labour camps. From 1942 on, the complex served as one of the main training facilities for female SS guards. Medical experiments were carried out on the women at Ravensbrück and in early

1945 the SS built a gas chamber, where approximately 5,000 to 6,000 prisoners were murdered. More than 100,000 women prisoners from all over Nazi-occupied Europe had passed through Ravensbrück before the Soviets liberated the camp on April 29-30, 1945. Approximately 50,000 women died in the camp.

Roma Also known as Romani. An ethnic group primarily located in central and eastern Europe. The Roma were commonly referred to as Gypsies in the past, a term now generally considered to be derogatory, and they have often lived on the fringes of society and been subject to persecution. During the Holocaust, which the Roma refer to in Romani as the *Porajmos* – the devouring – they were stripped of their citizenship under the Nuremberg Laws and were targeted for death under Hitler's race policies. The estimation of how many Roma were killed varies widely and has been difficult to document – estimations generally range between 200,000 and one million. *See also* Nuremberg Laws.

Royal Free City A designation afforded to major cities in the Kingdom of Hungary between the fifteenth and early twentieth century. The term signified both ties to the nobility as well as a certain amount of self-determination.

Shabbat (Hebrew; in English, Sabbath) The weekly day of rest beginning Friday at sunset and ending Saturday at sundown, ushered in by the lighting of candles on Friday night and the recitation of blessings over wine and challah (egg bread); a day of celebration as well as prayer, it is customary to eat three festive meals, attend synagogue services and refrain from doing any work or travelling.

shochet (Hebrew; in Yiddish, *shoykhet*) Ritual slaughterer. A man trained to slaughter animals painlessly and check that the product meets the various criteria of kosher slaughter. *See also* kosher.

SS (abbreviation of Schutzstaffel; Defence Corps) The SS was established in 1925 as Adolf Hitler's elite corps of personal bodyguards. Under the direction of Heinrich Himmler, its membership grew from 280 in 1929 to 50,000 when the Nazis came to power in 1933, and to nearly a quarter of a million on the eve of World War II. The SS was comprised of the Allgemeine-SS (General SS) and the Waffen-SS (Armed, or Combat SS). The General SS dealt with policing and the enforcement of Nazi racial policies in Germany and the Nazi-occupied countries. An important unit within the SS was the Reichssicherheitshauptamt (RSHA, the Central Office of Reich Security), whose responsibility included the Gestapo (Geheime Staatspolizei). The SS ran the concentration and death camps, with all their associated economic enterprises, and also fielded its own Waffen-SS military divisions, including some recruited from the occupied countries.

Star of David (in Hebrew, *Magen David*) The six-pointed star that is the ancient and most recognizable symbol of Judaism. During World War II, Jews in Nazi-occupied areas were frequently forced to wear a badge or armband with the Star of David on it as an identifying mark of their lesser status and to single them out as targets for persecution.

Theresienstadt (German; in Czech, Terezin) A walled town in the Czech Republic sixty kilometres north of Prague that served as both a ghetto and a concentration camp. More than 73,000 Jews from the German Protectorate of Bohemia and Moravia and from the Greater German Reich (including Austria and parts of Poland) were deported to Theresienstadt between 1941 and 1945, 60,000 of whom were deported to Auschwitz or other death camps. Theresienstadt was showcased as a "model" ghetto for propaganda purposes to demonstrate to delegates from the International Red Cross and others the "humane" treatment of Jews and to counter information reaching the Allies about Nazi atrocities and mass murder. Theresienstadt was liberated on May 8, 1945 by the Soviet Red Army.

Torah (Hebrew) The Five Books of Moses (the first five books of the Bible); also called the Pentateuch. The Torah is the core of Jewish scripture, traditionally believed to have been given to Moses on

Mount Sinai. In Christianity it is referred to as the "Old Testament."

Wallenberg, Raoul (1912–1947?) The Swedish diplomat who was sent to Hungary in June 1944 by the US Refugee Board and succeeded in saving tens of thousands of Budapest Jews by issuing them Swedish certificates of protection. The Swedish government also authorized Wallenberg to set up thirty "safe houses" and organize food distribution, medical assistance and child care for Jews in Budapest. Of the slightly more than 100,000 Jews who remained alive in Budapest at the end of the war (out of a pre-war population of 247,000), the majority were saved through his efforts. Wallenberg was awarded the title of Righteous Among the Nations by Yad Vashem in 1986 and has been honoured by memorials or monuments in ten other countries.

Yiddish A language derived from Middle High German with elements of Hebrew, Aramaic, Romance and Slavic languages, and written in Hebrew characters. Spoken by Jews in east-central Europe for roughly a thousand years from the tenth century to the mid-twentieth century, it was still the most common language among European Jews until the outbreak of World War II. There are similarities between Yiddish and contemporary German.

Zionism A movement promoted by the Viennese Jewish journalist Theodor Herzl, who argued in his 1896 book *Der Judenstaat* (The Jewish State) that the best way to resolve the problem of antisemitism and persecution of Jews in Europe was to create an independent Jewish state in the historic Jewish homeland of Biblical Israel. Zionists also promoted the revival of Hebrew as a Jewish national language.

Leslie Meisels: Photographs

1   Leslie Meisels at one-and-a-half. Nádudvar, 1928.

2   Leslie, age three, 1930.

3   The Meisels brothers in 1938. From left to right: George, Leslie and Frank.

4   Leslie's only photo of his paternal grandmother, taken while they were visiting their extended family before the war. Back row, left to right: Leslie's great-aunt, Emma; his brother Frank; Leslie; and his cousin Magda. Front row, left to right: Leslie's grandmother; his cousin Pista; and Leslie's great-aunt Juliska.

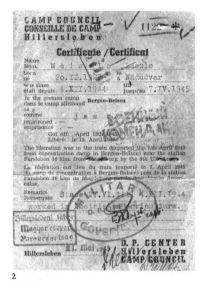

1

2

3

1 & 2 The identity papers issued to Leslie by the American Army after his liberation. Hillersleben, June 1945.

3 The Meisels family in their backyard soon after reuniting. Leslie is standing at the back. Left to right in front: Frank; Etelka and Lajos Meisels; and George. Nádudvar, 1945.

1 Leslie, age twenty-one. 1948.
2 Leslie in Austria, while waiting for his visa to the US. 1958.
3 The Meisels brothers, circa 1955. From left to right: Frank, George and Leslie.

1 Leslie and Eva (née Silber), with their parents, celebrating the couple's engagement. From left to right: Leslie's mother, Etelka, his father, Lajos, Eva, Leslie, and Eva's parents Irene and Erno Sugar. November 1960.

2 Leslie and Eva's engagement photo. November 26, 1960.

Leslie and Eva's wedding. May 1961.

1 The Meisels' daughters, Judy (left) and Edith (right). Toronto, 1970.
2 The Meisels family in front of their Toronto home, 1988. From left to right: Judy, Eva, Leslie and Edith.

1 Frank (left) with Leslie at Judy's wedding. August 29, 2004.

2 Edith's graduation from law school. Left to right: Eva's father, Erno, Edith, Leslie, Eva and Judy. 1991.

1 Leslie and Eva celebrating Mother's Day with their children and grandchildren.
   Back row (left to right): Judy's husband, Stuart Levson; Edith's husband, Philip
   Dover; Edith; and Leslie. Front row (left to right): Judy, holding her son, Jordan;
   Edith's daughter Jessica; Eva; and Edith's daughter Rachel. Toronto, 2005.

2 Leslie and Eva on their fiftieth wedding anniversary, at the vow renewal celebration their children organized. Standing in back, left to right: Granddaughter
   Jessica, Edith, Philip, grandson Jordan, Judy, Stuart and granddaughter Jaimee. In
   front: Eva, Leslie, and granddaughter Rachel. May 2011.

Leslie's grandson, Jordan, with his grandfather. December 2006.

Leslie Meisels' honorary membership in the 30th Infantry Division Veterans of World War II, awarded after he was reunited with his liberators. Hudson Falls, NY, 2009.

In recognition and appreciation of

LESLIE MEISELS

Holocaust Survivor

April 26, 2010

On behalf of the Government of Ontario, I am honoured
to join Ontarians provincewide in paying solemn tribute to you for
your profound courage, strength and determination.

Few can fully comprehend the unspeakable suffering,
cruelty and inhumanity that you and your fellow Holocaust
survivors witnessed and endured.

Yours is a remarkable story, one that serves as a
compelling reminder of our obligation — as a society and as
individuals — to learn from the lessons of our history, to be vigilant against all
forms of hatred and intolerance, and to embrace inclusiveness and
diversity — in the laws of our land and in our hearts.

You are a role model, a hero, a true survivor.
Please accept my personal best wishes.

Dalton McGuinty
Premier

Leslie Meisels' certificate of recognition from the Ontario government and the Canadian Society for Yad Vashem, given in honour of his many achievements and his contribution to Holocaust education.

1 Leslie, second from left, is pictured with then Ontario Premier Dalton McGuinty (far left), MPP Eric Hoskins and MPP Monte Kwinter (far right). Toronto, April 26, 2010.

2 Leslie's daughter Edith in front of the house where he grew up. Nádudvar, 1991.

Eva Meisels: Photographs

1 Juliska and Adolf, Eva's maternal grandparents. Date unknown.
2 Wedding photo of Eva's parents, Erno and Irene Silber. Budapest, August 14, 1938.
3 Eva's paternal grandparents. Date unknown.

1 The Silber family outside their apartment building, circa 1940.
2 Eva, age one. Budapest, 1940.
3 Eva at approximately three years old.
4 Eva, age four, 1943.

1 Eva visiting her mother's family in Ibrány before the occupation. Back row (left to right): Eva's aunt Elisabeth; her uncle Ben (Bela); her mother, Irene; her aunt Jolan; Uncle Leonard (Lajos) and Aunt Olga. Eva is in the middle row with her grandparents, and in the front row are her mother's three youngest siblings. 1942.

2 A Chanukah party in Eva's nursery school. Eva, in the front row with a bow in her hair, is sitting beside the friends who were in the bomb shelter with her during the siege of Budapest. 1943.

3 Eva's father, Erno (back row, far right), in a forced labour group.

4 Erno Silber, circa 1942.

1 The Silber family at Aunt Olga's wedding after the war. Back row, left to right: Eva's parents, Irene and Erno; Aunt Olga; Uncle Josef; and Eva's paternal grandmother, Margaret. Seated in front are Uncle Alex (Sanyi) and his wife, Eta, with their first-born son, Zoli, and Eva. Budapest, 1948.

2 Eva and her parents after the war. Budapest, 1950.

3 Eva's grandmother, Margaret, who survived Auschwitz. Montreal, circa 1957.

4 Eva, age sixteen.

1 Eva and her parents soon after immigrating to Canada. Montreal, 1957.
2 Eva and Leslie on their wedding day, with Eva's mother's family. Montreal, 1961.
3 Eva's mother, Irene (seated), with the four siblings who survived the war. Left to right: Bözsi, Leonard, Ben and Olga.
4 Eva with her father, Erno Sugar, on his eightieth birthday. Toronto, 1993.

Index

The Azrieli Foundation was established in 1989 to realize and extend the philanthropic vision of David J. Azrieli, C.M., C.Q., M.Arch. The Foundation's mission is to support a wide spectrum of initiatives in education and research. The Azrieli Foundation is an active supporter of programs in the fields of Education, the education of architects, scientific and medical research, and the arts. The Azrieli Foundation's many initiatives include: the Holocaust Survivor Memoirs Program, which collects, preserves, publishes and distributes the written memoirs of survivors in Canada; the Azrieli Institute for Educational Empowerment, an innovative program successfully working to keep at-risk youth in school; the Azrieli Fellows Program, which promotes academic excellence and leadership on the graduate level at Israeli universities; the Azrieli Music Project, which celebrates and fosters the creation of high-quality new Jewish orchestral music; and the Azrieli Neurodevelopmental Research Program, which supports advanced research on neurodevelopmental disorders, particularly Fragile X and Autism Spectrum Disorders.